Hadoop Essentials

Delve into the key concepts of Hadoop and get a
thorough understanding of the Hadoop ecosystem

Shiva Achari

PUBLISHING

BIRMINGHAM - MUMBAI

Hadoop Essentials

First published: April 2015

Production reference: 1240415

Published by Packt Publishing Ltd.
Livery Place
35 Livery Street
Birmingham B3 2PB, UK.

ISBN 978-1-78439-668-8

www.packtpub.com

Credits

Author

Shiva Achari

Reviewers

Anindita Basak

Ralf Becher

Marius Danciu

Dmitry Spikhalskiy

Commissioning Editor

Sarah Crofton

Acquisition Editor

Subho Gupta

Content Development Editor

Rahul Nair

Technical Editor

Bharat Patil

Copy Editors

Hiral Bhat

Charlotte Carneiro

Puja Lalwani

Sonia Mathur

Kriti Sharma

Sameen Siddiqui

Project Coordinator

Leena Purkait

Proofreaders

Simran Bhogal

Safis Editing

Linda Morris

Indexer

Priya Sane

Graphics

Sheetal Aute

Jason Monteiro

Production Coordinator

Komal Ramchandani

Cover Work

Komal Ramchandani

About the Author

Shiva Achari has over 8 years of extensive industry experience and is currently working as a Big Data Architect consultant with companies such as Oracle and Teradata. Over the years, he has architected, designed, and developed multiple innovative and high-performance large-scale solutions, such as distributed systems, data centers, big data management tools, SaaS cloud applications, Internet applications, and Data Analytics solutions.

He is also experienced in designing big data and analytics applications, such as ingestion, cleansing, transformation, correlation of different sources, data mining, and user experience in Hadoop, Cassandra, Solr, Storm, R, and Tableau.

He specializes in developing solutions for the big data domain and possesses sound hands-on experience on projects migrating to the Hadoop world, new developments, product consulting, and POC. He also has hands-on expertise in technologies such as Hadoop, Yarn, Sqoop, Hive, Pig, Flume, Solr, Lucene, Elasticsearch, Zookeeper, Storm, Redis, Cassandra, HBase, MongoDB, Talend, R, Mahout, Tableau, Java, and J2EE.

He has been involved in reviewing *Mastering Hadoop, Packt Publishing*.

Shiva has expertise in requirement analysis, estimations, technology evaluation, and system architecture along with domain experience in telecoms, Internet applications, document management, healthcare, and media.

Currently, he is supporting presales activities such as writing technical proposals (RFP), providing technical consultation to customers, and managing deliveries of big data practice groups in Teradata.

He is active on his LinkedIn page at http://in.linkedin.com/in/shivaachari/.

Acknowledgments

I would like to dedicate this book to my family, especially my father, mother, and wife. My father is my role model and I cannot find words to thank him enough, and I'm missing him as he passed away last year. My wife and mother have supported me throughout my life. I'd also like to dedicate this book to a special one whom we are expecting this July. Packt Publishing has been very kind and supportive, and I would like to thank all the individuals who were involved in editing, reviewing, and publishing this book. Some of the content was taken from my experiences, research, studies, and from the audiences of some of my trainings. I would like to thank my audience who found the book worth reading and hope that you gain the knowledge and help and implement them in your projects.

About the Reviewers

Anindita Basak is working as a big data cloud consultant and trainer and is highly enthusiastic about core Apache Hadoop, vendor-specific Hadoop distributions, and the Hadoop open source ecosystem. She works as a specialist in a big data start-up in the Bay area and with fortune brand clients across the U.S. She has been playing with Hadoop on Azure from the days of its incubation (that is, www.hadooponazure.com). Previously in her role, she has worked as a module lead for Alten Group Company and in the Azure Pro Direct Delivery group for Microsoft. She has also worked as a senior software engineer on the implementation and migration of various enterprise applications on Azure Cloud in the healthcare, retail, and financial domain. She started her journey with Microsoft Azure in the Microsoft Cloud Integration Engineering (CIE) team and worked as a support engineer for Microsoft India (R&D) Pvt. Ltd.

With more than 7 years of experience with the Microsoft .NET, Java, and the Hadoop technology stack, she is solely focused on the big data cloud and data science. She is a technical speaker, active blogger, and conducts various training programs on the Hortonworks and Cloudera developer/administrative certification programs. As an MVB, she loves to share her technical experience and expertise through her blog at http://anindita9.wordpress.com and http://anindita9.azurewebsites.net. You can get a deeper insight into her professional life on her LinkedIn page, and you can follow her on Twitter. Her Twitter handle is @imcuteani.

She recently worked as a technical reviewer for *HDInsight Essentials (volume I and II)* and *Microsoft Tabular Modeling Cookbook*, both by Packt Publishing.

Ralf Becher has worked as an IT system architect and data management consultant for more than 15 years in the areas of banking, insurance, logistics, automotive, and retail.

He is specialized in modern, quality-assured data management. He has been helping customers process, evaluate, and maintain the quality of the company data by helping them introduce, implement, and improve complex solutions in the fields of data architecture, data integration, data migration, master data management, metadata management, data warehousing, and business intelligence.

He started working with big data on Hadoop in 2012. He runs his BI and data integration blog at `http://irregular-bi.tumblr.com/`.

Marius Danciu has over 15 years of experience in developing and architecting Java platform server-side applications in the data synchronization and big data analytics fields. He's very fond of the Scala programming language and functional programming concepts and finding its applicability in everyday work. He is the coauthor of *The Definitive Guide to Lift*, Apress.

Dmitry Spikhalskiy is currently holding the position of a software engineer at the Russian social network, Odnoklassniki, and working on a search engine, video recommendation system, and movie content analysis.

Previously, he took part in developing the Mind Labs' platform and its infrastructure, and benchmarks for high load video conference and streaming services, which got "The biggest online-training in the world" Guinness World Record. More than 12,000 people participated in this competition. He also a mobile social banking start-up called Instabank as its technical lead and architect. He has also reviewed *Learning Google Guice, PostgreSQL 9 Admin Cookbook*, and *Hadoop MapReduce v2 Cookbook*, all by Packt Publishing.

He graduated from Moscow State University with an MSc degree in computer science, where he first got interested in parallel data processing, high load systems, and databases.

www.PacktPub.com

Support files, eBooks, discount offers, and more

For support files and downloads related to your book, please visit www.PacktPub.com.

Did you know that Packt offers eBook versions of every book published, with PDF and ePub files available? You can upgrade to the eBook version at www.PacktPub.com and as a print book customer, you are entitled to a discount on the eBook copy. Get in touch with us at service@packtpub.com for more details.

At www.PacktPub.com, you can also read a collection of free technical articles, sign up for a range of free newsletters and receive exclusive discounts and offers on Packt books and eBooks.

https://www2.packtpub.com/books/subscription/packtlib

Do you need instant solutions to your IT questions? PacktLib is Packt's online digital book library. Here, you can search, access, and read Packt's entire library of books.

Why subscribe?

- Fully searchable across every book published by Packt
- Copy and paste, print, and bookmark content
- On demand and accessible via a web browser

Free access for Packt account holders

If you have an account with Packt at www.PacktPub.com, you can use this to access PacktLib today and view 9 entirely free books. Simply use your login credentials for immediate access.

Table of Contents

Preface

Hadoop is quite a fascinating and interesting project that has seen quite a lot of interest and contributions from the various organizations and institutions. Hadoop has come a long way, from being a batch processing system to a data lake and high-volume streaming analysis in low latency with the help of various Hadoop ecosystem components, specifically YARN. This progress has been substantial and has made Hadoop a powerful system, which can be designed as a storage, transformation, batch processing, analytics, or streaming and real-time processing system.

Hadoop project as a data lake can be divided in multiple phases such as data ingestion, data storage, data access, data processing, and data management. For each phase, we have different sub-projects that are tools, utilities, or frameworks to help and accelerate the process. The Hadoop ecosystem components are tested, configurable and proven and to build similar utility on our own it would take a huge amount of time and effort to achieve. The core of the Hadoop framework is complex for development and optimization. The smart way to speed up and ease the process is to utilize different Hadoop ecosystem components that are very useful, so that we can concentrate more on the application flow design and integration with other systems.

With the emergence of many useful sub-projects in Hadoop and other tools within the Hadoop ecosystem, the question that arises is which tool to use when and how effectively. This book is intended to complete the jigsaw puzzle of when and how to use the various ecosystem components, and to make you well aware of the Hadoop ecosystem utilities and the cases and scenarios where they should be used.

What this book covers

Chapter 1, Introduction to Big Data and Hadoop, covers an overview of big data and Hadoop, plus different use case patterns with advantages and features of Hadoop.

Chapter 2, Hadoop Ecosystem, explores the different phases or layers of Hadoop project development and some components that can be used in each layer.

Chapter 3, Pillars of Hadoop – HDFS, MapReduce, and YARN, is about the three key basic components of Hadoop, which are HDFS, MapReduce, and YARN.

Chapter 4, Data Access Components – Hive and Pig, covers the data access components Hive and Pig, which are abstract layers of the SQL-like and Pig Latin procedural languages, respectively, on top of the MapReduce framework.

Chapter 5, Storage Components – HBase, is about the NoSQL component database HBase in detail.

Chapter 6, Data Ingestion in Hadoop – Sqoop and Flume, covers the data ingestion library tools Sqoop and Flume.

Chapter 7, Streaming and Real-time Analysis – Storm and Spark, is about the streaming and real-time frameworks Storm and Spark built on top of YARN.

What you need for this book

A prerequisite for this book is good understanding of Java programming and basics of distributed computing will be very helpful and an interest to understand about Hadoop and its ecosystem components.

 The code and syntax have been tested in Hadoop 2.4.1 and other compatible ecosystem component versions, but may vary in the newer version.

Who this book is for

If you are a system or application developer interested in learning how to solve practical problems using the Hadoop framework, then this book is ideal for you. This book is also meant for Hadoop professionals who want to find solutions to the different challenges they come across in their Hadoop projects. It assumes a familiarity with distributed storage and distributed applications.

Conventions

In this book, you will find a number of text styles that distinguish between different kinds of information. Here are some examples of these styles and an explanation of their meaning.

Code words in text, database table names, folder names, filenames, file extensions, pathnames, dummy URLs, user input, and Twitter handles are shown as follows: "We can include other contexts through the use of the `include` directive."

A block of code is set as follows:

```
public static class MyPartitioner extends    org.apache.hadoop.
mapreduce.Partitioner<Text,Text>

{
  @Override
  public int getPartition(Text key, Text value, int numPartitions)
  {
   int count =Integer.parseInt(line[1]);
   if(count<=3)
    return 0;
   else
    return 1;
  }
}

And in Driver class
job.setPartitionerClass(MyPartitioner.class);
```

Any command-line input or output is written as follows:

```
hadoop fs -put /home/shiva/Samplefile.txt  /user/shiva/dir3/
```

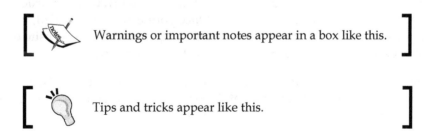

Warnings or important notes appear in a box like this.

Tips and tricks appear like this.

Reader feedback

Feedback from our readers is always welcome. Let us know what you think about this book—what you liked or disliked. Reader feedback is important for us as it helps us develop titles that you will really get the most out of.

To send us general feedback, simply e-mail feedback@packtpub.com, and mention the book's title in the subject of your message.

If there is a topic that you have expertise in and you are interested in either writing or contributing to a book, see our author guide at www.packtpub.com/authors.

Customer support

Now that you are the proud owner of a Packt book, we have a number of things to help you to get the most from your purchase.

Downloading the example code

You can download the example code files from your account at http://www.packtpub.com for all the Packt Publishing books you have purchased. If you purchased this book elsewhere, you can visit http://www.packtpub.com/support and register to have the files e-mailed directly to you.

Errata

Although we have taken every care to ensure the accuracy of our content, mistakes do happen. If you find a mistake in one of our books—maybe a mistake in the text or the code—we would be grateful if you could report this to us. By doing so, you can save other readers from frustration and help us improve subsequent versions of this book. If you find any errata, please report them by visiting http://www.packtpub.com/submit-errata, selecting your book, clicking on the **Errata Submission Form** link, and entering the details of your errata. Once your errata are verified, your submission will be accepted and the errata will be uploaded to our website or added to any list of existing errata under the Errata section of that title.

To view the previously submitted errata, go to https://www.packtpub.com/books/content/support and enter the name of the book in the search field. The required information will appear under the **Errata** section.

Piracy

Piracy of copyrighted material on the Internet is an ongoing problem across all media. At Packt, we take the protection of our copyright and licenses very seriously. If you come across any illegal copies of our works in any form on the Internet, please provide us with the location address or website name immediately so that we can pursue a remedy.

Please contact us at `copyright@packtpub.com` with a link to the suspected pirated material.

We appreciate your help in protecting our authors and our ability to bring you valuable content.

Questions

If you have a problem with any aspect of this book, you can contact us at `questions@packtpub.com`, and we will do our best to address the problem.

1
Introduction to Big Data and Hadoop

Hello big data enthusiast! By this time, I am sure you must have heard a lot about big data, as big data is the hot IT buzzword and there is a lot of excitement about big data. Let us try to understand the necessities of big data. There are humungous amount of data, available on the Internet, at institutions, and with some organizations, which have a lot of meaningful insights, which can be analyzed using data science techniques and involves complex algorithms. Data science techniques require a lot of processing time, intermediate data(s), and CPU power, that may take roughly tens of hours on gigabytes of data and data science works on a trial and error basis, to check if an algorithm can process the data better or not to get such insights. Big data systems can process data analytics not only faster but also efficiently for a large data and can enhance the scope of R&D analysis and can yield more meaningful insights and faster than any other analytic or BI system.

Big data systems have emerged due to some issues and limitations in traditional systems. The traditional systems are good for **Online Transaction Processing (OLTP)** and **Business Intelligence (BI)**, but are not easily scalable considering cost, effort, and manageability aspect. Processing heavy computations are difficult and prone to memory issues, or will be very slow, which hinders data analysis to a greater extent. Traditional systems lack extensively in data science analysis and make big data systems powerful and interesting. Some examples of big data use cases are predictive analytics, fraud analytics, machine learning, identifying patterns, data analytics, semi-structured, and unstructured data processing and analysis.

V's of big data

Typically, the problem that comes in the bracket of big data is defined by terms that are often called as V's of big data. There are typically three V's, which are Volume, Velocity, and variety, as shown in the following image:

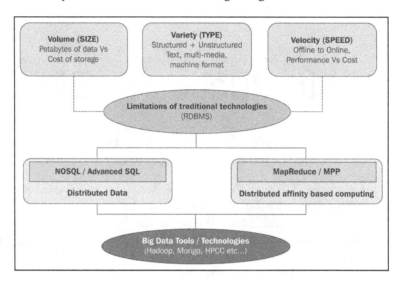

Volume

According to the fifth annual survey by **International Data Corporation (IDC)**, 1.8 zettabytes (1.8 trillion gigabytes) of information were created and replicated in 2011 alone, which is up from 800 GB in 2009, and the number is expected to more than double every two years surpassing 35 zettabytes by 2020. Big data systems are designed to store these amounts of data and even beyond that too with a fault tolerant architecture, and as it is distributed and replicated across multiple nodes, the underlying nodes can be average computing systems, which too need not be high performing systems, which reduces the cost drastically.

The cost per terabyte storage in big data is very less than in other systems, and this has made organizations interested to a greater extent, and even if the data grows multiple times, it is easily scalable, and nodes can be added without much maintenance effort.

Velocity

Processing and analyzing the amount of data that we discussed earlier is one of the key interest areas where big data is gaining popularity and has grown enormously. Not all data to be processed has to be larger in volume initially, but as we process and execute some complex algorithms, the data can grow massively. For processing most of the algorithms, we would require intermediate or temporary data, which can be in GB or TB for big data, so while processing, we would require some significant amount of data, and processing also has to be faster. Big data systems can process huge complex algorithms on huge data much quickly, as it leverages parallel processing across distributed environment, which executes multiple processes in parallel at the same time, and the job can be completed much faster.

For example, Yahoo created a world record in 2009 using Apache Hadoop for sorting a petabyte in 16.25 hours and a terabyte in 62 seconds. MapR have achieved terabyte data sorting in 55 seconds, which speaks volume for the processing power, especially in analytics where we need to use a lot of intermediate data to perform heavy time and memory intensive algorithms much faster.

Variety

Another big challenge for the traditional systems is to handle different variety of semi-structured data or unstructured data such as e-mails, audio and video analysis, image analysis, social media, gene, geospatial, 3D data, and so on. Big data can not only help store, but also utilize and process such data using algorithms much more quickly and also efficiently. Semi-structured and unstructured data processing is complex, and big data can use the data with minimal or no preprocessing like other systems and can save a lot of effort and help minimize loss of data.

Understanding big data

Actually, big data is a terminology which refers to challenges that we are facing due to exponential growth of data in terms of V problems. The challenges can be subdivided into the following phases:

- Capture
- Storage
- Search
- Sharing
- Analytics
- Visualization

Big data systems refer to technologies that can process and analyze data, which we discussed as volume, velocity, and variety data problems. The technologies that can solve big data problems should use the following architectural strategy:

- Distributed computing system
- Massively parallel processing (MPP)
- NoSQL (Not only SQL)
- Analytical database

The structure is as follows:

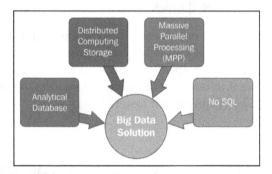

Big data systems use distributed computing and parallel processing to handle big data problems. Apart from distributed computing and MPP, there are other architectures that can solve big data problems that are toward database environment based system, which are NoSQL and Advanced SQL.

NoSQL

A NoSQL database is a widely adapted technology due to the schema less design, and its ability to scale up vertically and horizontally is fairly simple and in much less effort. SQL and RDBMS have ruled for more than three decades, and it performs well within the limits of the processing environment, and beyond that the RDBMS system performance degrades, cost increases, and manageability decreases, we can say that NoSQL provides an edge over RDBMS in these scenarios.

One important thing to mention is that NoSQLs do not support all ACID properties and are highly scalable, provide availability, and are also fault tolerant. NoSQL usually provides either consistency or availability (availability of nodes for processing), depending upon the architecture and design.

Types of NoSQL databases

As the NoSQL databases are nonrelational they have different sets of possible architecture and design. Broadly, there are four general types of NoSQL databases, based on how the data is stored:

1. **Key-value store**: These databases are designed for storing data in a key-value store. The key can be custom, can be synthetic, or can be autogenerated, and the value can be complex objects such as XML, JSON, or BLOB. Key of data is indexed for faster access to the data and improving the retrieval of value. Some popular key-value type databases are DynamoDB, Azure Table Storage (ATS), Riak, and BerkeleyDB.

2. **Column store**: These databases are designed for storing data as a group of column families. Read/write operation is done using columns, rather than rows. One of the advantages is the scope of compression, which can efficiently save space and avoid memory scan of the column. Due to the column design, not all files are required to be scanned, and each column file can be compressed, especially if a column has many nulls and repeating values. A column stores databases that are highly scalable and have very high performance architecture. Some popular column store type databases are HBase, BigTable, Cassandra, Vertica, and Hypertable.

3. **Document database**: These databases are designed for storing, retrieving, and managing document-oriented information. A document database expands on the idea of key-value stores where values or documents are stored using some structure and are encoded in formats such as XML, YAML, or JSON, or in binary forms such as BSON, PDF, Microsoft Office documents (MS Word, Excel), and so on. The advantage in storing in an encoded format like XML or JSON is that we can search with the key within the document of a data, and it is quite useful in ad hoc querying and semi-structured data. Some popular document-type databases are MongoDB and CouchDB.

4. **Graph database**: These databases are designed for data whose relations are well represented as trees or a graph, and has elements, usually with nodes and edges, which are interconnected. Relational databases are not so popular in performing graph-based queries as they require a lot of complex joins, and thus managing the interconnection becomes messy. Graph theoretic algorithms are useful for prediction, user tracking, clickstream analysis, calculating the shortest path, and so on, which will be processed by graph databases much more efficiently as the algorithms themselves are complex. Some popular graph-type databases are Neo4J and Polyglot.

Analytical database

An analytical database is a type of database built to store, manage, and consume big data. Analytical databases are vendor-managed DBMS, which are optimized for processing advanced analytics that involves highly complex queries on terabytes of data and complex statistical processing, data mining, and NLP (natural language processing). Examples of analytical databases are Vertica (acquired by HP), Aster Data (acquired by Teradata), Greenplum (acquired by EMC), and so on.

Who is creating big data?

Data is growing exponentially, and comes from multiple sources that are emitting data continuously and consistently. In some domains, we have to analyze the data that are processed by machines, sensors, quality, equipment, data points, and so on. A list of some sources that are creating big data is mentioned as follows:

- Monitoring sensors: Climate or ocean wave monitoring sensors generate data consistently and in a good size, and there would be more than millions of sensors that capture data.

- Posts to social media sites: Social media websites such as Facebook, Twitter, and others have a huge amount of data in petabytes.

- Digital pictures and videos posted online: Websites such as YouTube, Netflix, and others process a huge amount of digital videos and data that can be petabytes.

- Transaction records of online purchases: E-commerce sites such as eBay, Amazon, Flipkart, and others process thousands of transactions on a single time.

- Server/application logs: Applications generate log data that grows consistently, and analysis on these data becomes difficult.

- CDR (call data records): Roaming data and cell phone GPS signals to name a few.

- Science, genomics, biogeochemical, biological, and other complex and/or interdisciplinary scientific research.

Big data use cases

Let's look at the credit card issuer (use case demonstrated by MapR).

A credit card issuer client wants to improve the existing recommendation system that is lagging and can have potentially huge profits if recommendations can be faster.

The existing system is an **Enterprise Data Warehouse** (**EDW**), which is very costly and slower in generating recommendations, which, in turn, impacts on potential profits. As Hadoop is cheaper and faster, it will generate huge profits than the existing system.

Usually, a credit card customer will have data like the following:

- Customer purchase history (big)
- Merchant designations
- Merchant special offers

Let's analyze a general comparison of existing EDW platforms with a big data solution. The recommendation system is designed using Mahout (scalable Machine Learning library API) and Solr/Lucene. Recommendation is based on the co-occurrence matrix implemented as the search index.

The time improvement benchmarked was from 20 hours to just 3 hours, which is unbelievably six times less, as shown in the following image:

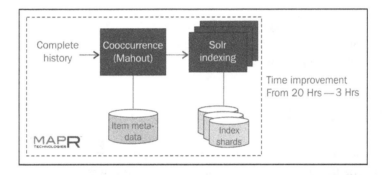

In the web tier in the following image, we can see that the improvement is from 8 hours to 3 minutes:

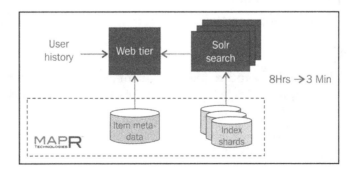

So, eventually, we can say that time decreases, revenue increases, and Hadoop offers a cost-effective solution, hence profit increases, as shown in the following image:

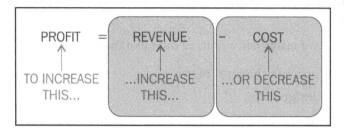

Big data use case patterns

There are many technological scenarios, and some of them are similar in pattern. It is a good idea to map scenarios with architectural patterns. Once these patterns, are understood, they become the fundamental building blocks of solutions. We will discuss five types of patterns in the following section.

 This solution is not always optimized, and it may depend on domain data, type of data, or some other factors. These examples are to visualize a problem and they can help to find a solution.

Big data as a storage pattern

Big data systems can be used as a storage pattern or as a data warehouse, where data from multiple sources, even with different types of data, can be stored and can be utilized later. The usage scenario and use case are as follows:

- Usage scenario:
    - Data getting continuously generated in large volumes
    - Need for preprocessing before getting loaded into the target system
- Use case:
    - Machine data capture for subsequent cleansing can be merged in multiple or single big file(s) and can be loaded in a Hadoop to compute
    - Unstructured data across multiple sources should be captured for subsequent analysis on emerging patterns

      °   Data loaded in Hadoop should be processed and filtered, and depending on the data, we can have the storage as a data warehouse, Hadoop, or any NoSQL system.

The storage pattern is shown in the following figure:

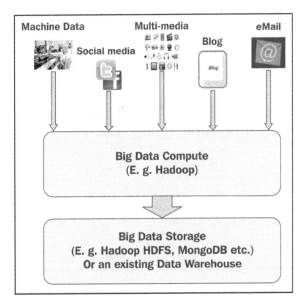

Big data as a data transformation pattern

Big data systems can be designed to perform transformation as the data loading and cleansing activity, and many transformations can be done faster than traditional systems due to parallelism. Transformation is one phase in the Extract–Transform–Load of data ingestion and cleansing phase. The usage scenario and use case are as follows:

- Usage scenario
    - ° A large volume of raw data to be preprocessed
    - ° Data type includes structured as well as non-structured data

- Use case
    - ° Evolution of ETL (Extract–Transform–Load) tools to leverage big data, for example, Pentaho, Talend, and so on. Also, in Hadoop, ELT (Extract–Load–Transform) is also trending, as the loading will be faster in Hadoop, and cleansing can run a parallel process to clean and transform the input, which will be faster

The data transformation pattern is shown in the following figure:

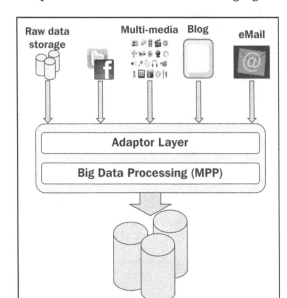

Big data for a data analysis pattern

Data analytics is of wider interest in big data systems, where a huge amount of data can be analyzed to generate statistical reports and insights about the data, which can be useful in business and understanding of patterns. The usage scenario and use case are as follows:

- Usage scenario
    - Improved response time for detection of patterns
    - Data analysis for non-structured data
- Use case
    - Fast turnaround for machine data analysis (for example, analysis of seismic data)
    - Pattern detection across structured and non-structured data (for example, fraud analysis)

Big data for data in a real-time pattern

Big data systems integrating with some streaming libraries and systems are capable of handling high scale real-time data processing. Real-time processing for a large and complex requirement possesses a lot of challenges such as performance, scalability, availability, resource management, low latency, and so on. Some streaming technologies such as Storm and Spark Streaming can be integrated with YARN. The usage scenario and use case are as follows:

- Usage scenario
    - Managing the action to be taken based on continuously changing data in real time

- Use case
    - Automated process control based on real time from manufacturing equipments
    - Real-time changes to plant operations based on events from business systems **Enterprise Resource Planning** (**ERPs**)

The data in a real-time pattern is shown in the following figure:

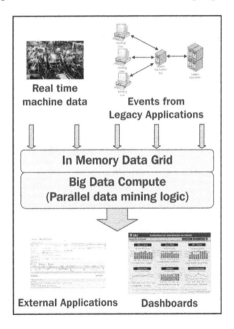

Big data for a low latency caching pattern

Big data systems can be tuned as a special case for a low latency system, where reads are much higher and updates are low, which can fetch the data faster and can be stored in memory, which can further improve the performance and avoid overheads. The usage scenario and use case are as follows:

- Usage scenario
    - Reads are far higher in ratio to writes
    - Reads require very low latency and a guaranteed response
    - Distributed location-based data caching

- Use case
    - Order promising solutions
    - Cloud-based identity and SSO
    - Low latency real-time personalized offers on mobile

The low latency caching pattern is shown in the following pattern:

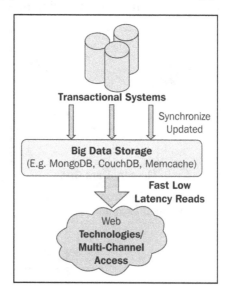

Some of the technology stacks that are widely used according to the layer and framework are shown in the following image:

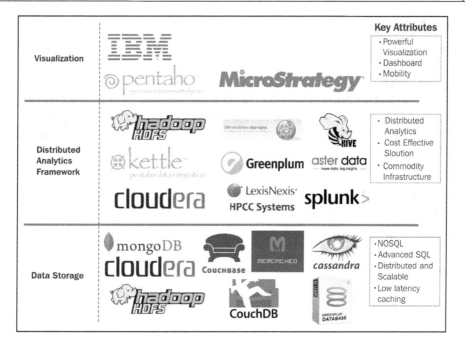

Hadoop

In big data, the most widely used system is Hadoop. Hadoop is an open source implementation of big data, which is widely accepted in the industry, and benchmarks for Hadoop are impressive and, in some cases, incomparable to other systems. Hadoop is used in the industry for large-scale, massively parallel, and distributed data processing. Hadoop is highly fault tolerant and configurable to as many levels as we need for the system to be fault tolerant, which has a direct impact to the number of times the data is stored across.

As we have already touched upon big data systems, the architecture revolves around two major components: distributed computing and parallel processing. In Hadoop, the distributed computing is handled by HDFS, and parallel processing is handled by MapReduce. In short, we can say that Hadoop is a combination of HDFS and MapReduce, as shown in the following image:

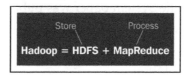

We will cover the above mentioned two topics in detail in the next chapters.

Hadoop history

Hadoop began from a project called Nutch, an open source crawler-based search, which processes on a distributed system. In 2003–2004, Google released Google MapReduce and GFS papers. MapReduce was adapted on Nutch. Doug Cutting and Mike Cafarella are the creators of Hadoop. When Doug Cutting joined Yahoo, a new project was created along the similar lines of Nutch, which we call Hadoop, and Nutch remained as a separate sub-project. Then, there were different releases, and other separate sub-projects started integrating with Hadoop, which we call a Hadoop ecosystem.

The following figure and description depicts the history with timelines and milestones achieved in Hadoop:

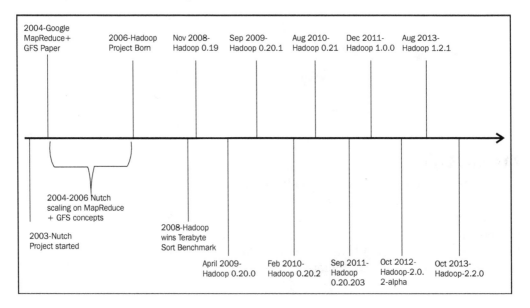

Description

- **2002.8**: The Nutch Project was started
- **2003.2**: The first MapReduce library was written at Google
- **2003.10**: The Google File System paper was published
- **2004.12**: The Google MapReduce paper was published
- **2005.7**: Doug Cutting reported that Nutch now uses new MapReduce implementation
- **2006.2**: Hadoop code moved out of Nutch into a new Lucene sub-project

- **2006.11**: The Google Bigtable paper was published
- **2007.2**: The first HBase code was dropped from Mike Cafarella
- **2007.4**: Yahoo! Running Hadoop on 1000-node cluster
- **2008.1**: Hadoop made an Apache Top Level Project
- **2008.7**: Hadoop broke the Terabyte data sort Benchmark
- **2008.11**: Hadoop 0.19 was released
- **2011.12**: Hadoop 1.0 was released
- **2012.10**: Hadoop 2.0 was alpha released
- **2013.10**: Hadoop 2.2.0 was released
- **2014.10**: Hadoop 2.6.0 was released

Advantages of Hadoop

Hadoop has a lot of advantages, and some of them are as follows:

- **Low cost — Runs on commodity hardware:** Hadoop can run on average performing commodity hardware and doesn't require a high performance system, which can help in controlling cost and achieve scalability and performance. Adding or removing nodes from the cluster is simple, as an when we require. The cost per terabyte is lower for storage and processing in Hadoop.

- **Storage flexibility**: Hadoop can store data in raw format in a distributed environment. Hadoop can process the unstructured data and semi-structured data better than most of the available technologies. Hadoop gives full flexibility to process the data and we will not have any loss of data.

- **Open source community:** Hadoop is open source and supported by many contributors with a growing network of developers worldwide. Many organizations such as Yahoo, Facebook, Hortonworks, and others have contributed immensely toward the progress of Hadoop and other related sub-projects.

- **Fault tolerant**: Hadoop is massively scalable and fault tolerant. Hadoop is reliable in terms of data availability, and even if some nodes go down, Hadoop can recover the data. Hadoop architecture assumes that nodes can go down and the system should be able to process the data.

- **Complex data analytics**: With the emergence of big data, data science has also grown leaps and bounds, and we have complex and heavy computation intensive algorithms for data analysis. Hadoop can process such scalable algorithms for a very large-scale data and can process the algorithms faster.

Uses of Hadoop

Some examples of use cases where Hadoop is used are as follows:

- Searching/text mining
- Log processing
- Recommendation systems
- Business intelligence/data warehousing
- Video and image analysis
- Archiving
- Graph creation and analysis
- Pattern recognition
- Risk assessment
- Sentiment analysis

Hadoop ecosystem

A Hadoop cluster can be of thousands of nodes, and it is complex and difficult to manage manually, hence there are some components that assist configuration, maintenance, and management of the whole Hadoop system. In this book, we will touch base upon the following components in *Chapter 2, Hadoop Ecosystem*.

Layer	Utility/Tool name
Distributed filesystem	Apache HDFS
Distributed programming	Apache MapReduce
	Apache Hive
	Apache Pig
	Apache Spark
NoSQL databases	Apache HBase
Data ingestion	Apache Flume
	Apache Sqoop
	Apache Storm
Service programming	Apache Zookeeper
Scheduling	Apache Oozie
Machine learning	Apache Mahout
System deployment	Apache Ambari

All the components above are helpful in managing Hadoop tasks and jobs.

Apache Hadoop

The open source Hadoop is maintained by the Apache Software Foundation. The official website for Apache Hadoop is `http://hadoop.apache.org/`, where the packages and other details are described elaborately. The current Apache Hadoop project (version 2.6) includes the following modules:

- **Hadoop common**: The common utilities that support other Hadoop modules
- **Hadoop Distributed File System (HDFS)**: A distributed filesystem that provides high-throughput access to application data
- **Hadoop YARN**: A framework for job scheduling and cluster resource management
- **Hadoop MapReduce**: A YARN-based system for parallel processing of large datasets

Apache Hadoop can be deployed in the following three modes:

- **Standalone**: It is used for simple analysis or debugging.
- **Pseudo distributed**: It helps you to simulate a multi-node installation on a single node. In pseudo-distributed mode, each of the component processes runs in a separate JVM. Instead of installing Hadoop on different servers, you can simulate it on a single server.
- **Distributed**: Cluster with multiple worker nodes in tens or hundreds or thousands of nodes.

In a Hadoop ecosystem, along with Hadoop, there are many utility components that are separate Apache projects such as Hive, Pig, HBase, Sqoop, Flume, Zookeper, Mahout, and so on, which have to be configured separately. We have to be careful with the compatibility of subprojects with Hadoop versions as not all versions are inter-compatible.

Apache Hadoop is an open source project that has a lot of benefits as source code can be updated, and also some contributions are done with some improvements. One downside for being an open source project is that companies usually offer support for their products, not for an open source project. Customers prefer support and adapt Hadoop distributions supported by the vendors.

Let's look at some Hadoop distributions available.

Hadoop distributions

Hadoop distributions are supported by the companies managing the distribution, and some distributions have license costs also. Companies such as Cloudera, Hortonworks, Amazon, MapR, and Pivotal have their respective Hadoop distribution in the market that offers Hadoop with required sub-packages and projects, which are compatible and provide commercial support. This greatly reduces efforts, not just for operations, but also for deployment, monitoring, and tools and utility for easy and faster development of the product or project.

For managing the Hadoop cluster, Hadoop distributions provide some graphical web UI tooling for the deployment, administration, and monitoring of Hadoop clusters, which can be used to set up, manage, and monitor complex clusters, which reduce a lot of effort and time.

Some Hadoop distributions which are available are as follows:

- **Cloudera**: According to *The Forrester Wave™: Big Data Hadoop Solutions, Q1 2014*, this is the most widely used Hadoop distribution with the biggest customer base as it provides good support and has some good utility components such as Cloudera Manager, which can create, manage, and maintain a cluster, and manage job processing, and Impala is developed and contributed by Cloudera which has real-time processing capability.

- **Hortonworks**: Hortonworks' strategy is to drive all innovation through the open source community and create an ecosystem of partners that accelerates Hadoop adoption among enterprises. It uses an open source Hadoop project and is a major contributor to Hadoop enhancement in Apache Hadoop. Ambari was developed and contributed to Apache by Hortonworks. Hortonworks offers a very good, easy-to-use sandbox for getting started. Hortonworks contributed changes that made Apache Hadoop run natively on the Microsoft Windows platforms including Windows Server and Microsoft Azure.

- **MapR**: MapR distribution of Hadoop uses different concepts than plain open source Hadoop and its competitors, especially support for a network file system (NFS) instead of HDFS for better performance and ease of use. In NFS, Native Unix commands can be used instead of Hadoop commands. MapR have high availability features such as snapshots, mirroring, or stateful failover.

- **Amazon Elastic MapReduce (EMR)**: AWS's Elastic MapReduce (EMR) leverages its comprehensive cloud services, such as Amazon EC2 for compute, Amazon S3 for storage, and other services, to offer a very strong Hadoop solution for customers who wish to implement Hadoop in the cloud. EMR is much advisable to be used for infrequent big data processing. It might save you a lot of money.

Pillars of Hadoop

Hadoop is designed to be highly scalable, distributed, massively parallel processing, fault tolerant and flexible and the key aspect of the design are HDFS, MapReduce and YARN. HDFS and MapReduce can perform very large scale batch processing at a much faster rate. Due to contributions from various organizations and institutions Hadoop architecture has undergone a lot of improvements, and one of them is YARN. YARN has overcome some limitations of Hadoop and allows Hadoop to integrate with different applications and environments easily, especially in streaming and real-time analysis. One such example that we are going to discuss are Storm and Spark, they are well known in streaming and real-time analysis, both can integrate with Hadoop via YARN.

We will cover the concept of HDFS, MapReduce, and YARN in greater detail in *Chapter 3, Pillars of Hadoop – HDFS, MapReduce, and YARN*.

Data access components

MapReduce is a very powerful framework, but has a huge learning curve to master and optimize a MapReduce job. For analyzing data in a MapReduce paradigm, a lot of our time will be spent in coding. In big data, the users come from different backgrounds such as programming, scripting, EDW, DBA, analytics, and so on, for such users there are abstraction layers on top of MapReduce. Hive and Pig are two such layers, Hive has a SQL query-like interface and Pig has Pig Latin procedural language interface. Analyzing data on such layers becomes much easier.

We will cover the concept of Hive and Pig in greater detail in *Chapter 4, Data Access Component – Hive and Pig*.

Data storage component

HBase is a column store-based NoSQL database solution. HBase's data model is very similar to Google's BigTable framework. HBase can efficiently process random and real-time access in a large volume of data, usually millions or billions of rows. HBase's important advantage is that it supports updates on larger tables and faster lookup. The HBase data store supports linear and modular scaling. HBase stores data as a multidimensional map and is distributed. HBase operations are all MapReduce tasks that run in a parallel manner.

We will cover the concept of HBase in greater detail in *Chapter 5, Storage Component – HBase*.

Data ingestion in Hadoop

In Hadoop, storage is never an issue, but managing the data is the driven force around which different solutions can be designed differently with different systems, hence managing data becomes extremely critical. A better manageable system can help a lot in terms of scalability, reusability, and even performance. In a Hadoop ecosystem, we have two widely used tools: Sqoop and Flume, both can help manage the data and can import and export data efficiently, with a good performance. Sqoop is usually used for data integration with RDBMS systems, and Flume usually performs better with streaming log data.

We will cover the concept of Sqoop and Flume in greater detail in *Chapter 6, Data Ingestion in Hadoop – Sqoop and Flume*.

Streaming and real-time analysis

Storm and Spark are the two new fascinating components that can run on YARN and have some amazing capabilities in terms of processing streaming and real-time analysis. Both of these are used in scenarios where we have heavy continuous streaming data and have to be processed in, or near, real-time cases. The example which we discussed earlier for traffic analyzer is a good example for use cases of Storm and Spark.

We will cover the concept of Storm and Spark in greater detail in *Chapter 7, Streaming and Real-time Analysis – Storm and Spark*.

Summary

In this chapter, we spoke about the big data and its use case patterns. We explored a bit about Hadoop history, finally migrating to the advantages and uses of Hadoop.

Hadoop systems are complex to monitor and manage, and we have separate sub-projects' frameworks, tools, and utilities that integrate with Hadoop and help in better management of tasks, which are called a Hadoop ecosystem, and which we will be discussing in subsequent chapters.

Hadoop Ecosystem

2

Now that we have discussed and understood big data and Hadoop, we can move on to understanding the Hadoop ecosystem. A Hadoop cluster may have hundreds or thousands of nodes which are difficult to design, configure, and manage manually. Due to this, there arises a need for tools and utilities to manage systems and data easily and effectively. Along with Hadoop, we have separate sub-projects which are contributed by some organizations and contributors, and are managed mostly by Apache. The sub-projects integrate very well with Hadoop and can help us concentrate more on design and development rather than maintenance and monitoring, and can also help in the development and data management.

Before we understand different tools and technologies, let's understand a use case and how it differs from traditional systems.

Traditional systems

Traditional systems are good for OLTP (online transaction processing) and some basic Data Analysis and BI use cases. Within the scope, the traditional systems are best in performance and management. The following figure shows a traditional system on a high-level overview:

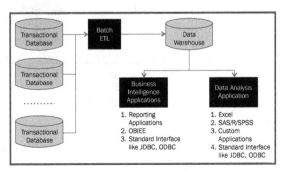

Traditional systems with BIA

The steps for typical traditional systems are as follows:

1. Data resides in a database
2. ETL (Extract Transform Load) processes
3. Data moved into a data warehouse
4. Business Intelligence Applications can have some BI reporting
5. Data can be used by Data Analysis Application as well

When the data grows, traditional systems fail to process, or even store, the data; and even if they do, it comes at a very high cost and effort because of the limitations in the architecture, issue with scalability and resource constraints, incapability or difficulty to scale horizontally.

Database trend

Database technologies have evolved over a period of time. We have RDBMS (relational database), EDW (Enterprise data warehouse), and now Hadoop and NoSQL-based database have emerged. Hadoop and NoSQL-based database are now the preferred technology used for the big data problems, and some traditional systems are gradually moving towards Hadoop and NoSQL, along with their existing systems. Some systems have different technologies to process the data such as, Hadoop with RDBMS, Hadoop with EDW, NoSQL with EDW, and NoSQL with Hadoop. The following figure depicts the database trend according to Forrester Research:

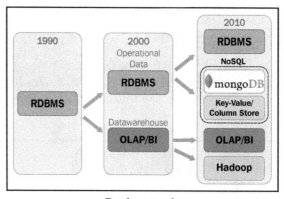

Database trends

The figure depicts the design trends and the technology which was available and adapted in a particular decade.

The 1990's decade was the RDBMS era which was designed for OLTP processing and data processing was not so complex.

The emergence and adaptation of data warehouse was in the 2000's, which is used for OLAP processing and BI.

From 2010 big data systems, especially Hadoop, have been adapted by many organizations to solve Big Data problems.

All these technologies can practically co-exist for a solution as each technology has its pros and cons because not all problems can be solved by any one technology.

The Hadoop use cases

Hadoop can help in solving the big data problems that we discussed in *Chapter 1, Introduction to Big Data and Hadoop*. Based on Data Velocity (Batch and Real time) and Data Variety (Structured, Semi-structured and Unstructured), we have different sets of use cases across different domains and industries. All these use cases are big data use cases and Hadoop can effectively help in solving them. Some use cases are depicted in the following figure:

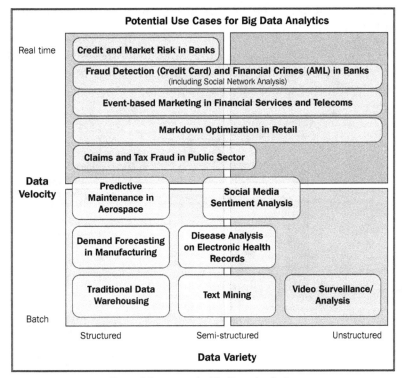

Potential use case for Big Data Analytics

Hadoop's basic data flow

A basic data flow of the Hadoop system can be divided into four phases:

1. **Capture Big Data** : The sources can be extensive lists that are structured, semi-structured, and unstructured, some streaming, real-time data sources, sensors, devices, machine-captured data, and many other sources. For data capturing and storage, we have different data integrators such as, Flume, Sqoop, Storm, and so on in the Hadoop ecosystem, depending on the type of data.

2. **Process and Structure**: We will be cleansing, filtering, and transforming the data by using a MapReduce-based framework or some other frameworks which can perform distributed programming in the Hadoop ecosystem. The frameworks available currently are MapReduce, Hive, Pig, Spark and so on.

3. **Distribute Results**: The processed data can be used by the BI and analytics system or the big data analytics system for performing analysis or visualization.

4. **Feedback and Retain**: The data analyzed can be fed back to Hadoop and used for improvements and audits.

The following figure shows the data captured and then processed in a Hadoop platform, and the results used in a Business Transactions and Interactions system, and a Business Intelligence and Analytics system:

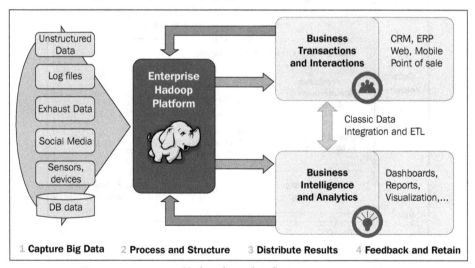

Hadoop basic data flow

Hadoop integration

Hadoop architecture is designed to be easily integrated with other systems. Integration is very important because although we can process the data efficiently in Hadoop, but we should also be able to send that result to another system to move the data to another level. Data has to be integrated with other systems to achieve interoperability and flexibility.

The following figure depicts the Hadoop system integrated with different systems and with some implemented tools for reference:

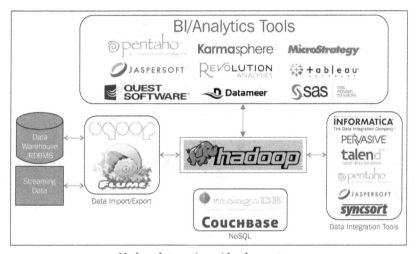

Hadoop Integration with other systems

Systems that are usually integrated with Hadoop are:

- Data Integration tools such as, Sqoop, Flume, and others
- NoSQL tools such as, Cassandra, MongoDB, Couchbase, and others
- ETL tools such as, Pentaho, Informatica, Talend, and others
- Visualization tools such as, Tableau, Sas, R, and others

The Hadoop ecosystem

The Hadoop ecosystem comprises of a lot of sub-projects and we can configure these projects as we need in a Hadoop cluster. As Hadoop is an open source software and has become popular, we see a lot of contributions and improvements supporting Hadoop by different organizations. All the utilities are absolutely useful and help in managing the Hadoop system efficiently. For simplicity, we will understand different tools by categorizing them.

The following figure depicts the layer, and the tools and utilities within that layer, in the Hadoop ecosystem:

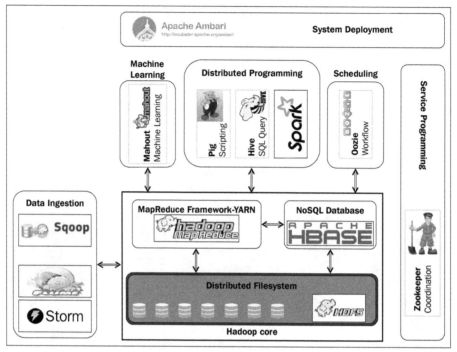

Hadoop ecosystem

Distributed filesystem

In Hadoop, we know that data is stored in a distributed computing environment, so the files are scattered across the cluster. We should have an efficient filesystem to manage the files in Hadoop. The filesystem used in Hadoop is HDFS, elaborated as Hadoop Distributed File System.

HDFS

HDFS is extremely scalable and fault tolerant. It is designed to efficiently process parallel processing in a distributed environment in even commodity hardware. HDFS has daemon processes in Hadoop, which manage the data. The processes are NameNode, DataNode, BackupNode, and Checkpoint NameNode.

We will discuss HDFS elaborately in the next chapter.

Distributed programming

To leverage the power of a distributed storage filesystem, Hadoop performs distributed programming which can do massive parallel programming. Distributed programming is the heart of any big data system, so it is extremely critical. The following are the different frameworks that can be used for distributed programming:

- MapReduce
- Hive
- Pig
- Spark

The basic layer in Hadoop for distributed programming is MapReduce. Let's introduce MapReduce:

- **Hadoop MapReduce**: MapReduce is the heart of the Hadoop system distributed programming. MapReduce is a framework model designed as parallel processing on a distributed environment. Hadoop MapReduce was inspired by Google MapReduce whitepaper. Hadoop MapReduce is scalable and massively parallel processing framework, which can work on huge data and is designed to run, even in commodity hardware. Before Hadoop 2.*x*, MapReduce was the only processing framework that could be performed, and then some utility extended and created a wrapper to program easily for faster development. We will discuss about Hadoop MapReduce in detail in *Chapter 3, Pillars of Hadoop – HDFS, MapReduce, and YARN*.

- **Apache Hive**: Hive provides a data warehouse infrastructure system for Hadoop, which creates a SQL-like wrapper interface called HiveQL, on top of MapReduce. Hive can be used to run some ad hoc querying and basic aggregation and summarization processing on the Hadoop data. HiveQL is not SQL92 compliant. Hive was developed by Facebook and contributed to Apache. Hive is designed on top of MapReduce, which means a HiveQL query will run the MapReduce jobs for processing the query. We can even extend HiveQL by using **User Defined Functions** (**UDF**).

- **Apache Pig**: Pig provides a scripting-like wrapper written in the Pig Latin language to process the data with script-like syntax. Pig was developed by Yahoo and contributed to Apache. Pig also translates the Pig Latin script code to MapReduce and executes the job. Pig is usually used for analyzing semi-structured and large data sets.

- **Apache Spark**: Spark provides a powerful alternative to Hadoop's MapReduce. Apache Spark is a parallel data processing framework that can run programs up to 100 times faster than Hadoop MapReduce in memory, or 10 times faster on disk. Spark is used for real-time stream processing and analysis of the data.

NoSQL databases

We have already discussed about NoSQL as one of the emerging and adopted systems. Within Hadoop ecosystem, we have a NoSQL database called HBase. HBase is one of the key component that provides a very flexible design and high volume simultaneous reads and write in low latency hence it is widely adopted.

Apache HBase

HBase is inspired from Google's Big Table. HBase is a sorted map, which is sparse, consistent, distributed, and multidimensional. HBase is a NoSQL, column oriented database and a key/value store, which works on top of HDFS. HBase provides faster lookup and also high volume inserts/updates of a random access request on a high scale. The HBase schema is very flexible and actually variable, where the columns can be added or removed at runtime. HBase supports low-latency and strongly consistent read and write operations. It is suitable for high-speed counter aggregation.

Many organizations or companies use HBase, such as Yahoo, Adobe, Facebook, Twitter, Stumbleupon, NGData, Infolinks, Trend Micro, and many more.

Data ingestion

Data management in big data is an important and critical aspect. We have to import and export large scale data to do processing, which becomes unmanageable in the production environment. In Hadoop, we deal with different set of sources such as batch, streaming, real time, and also sources that are complex in data formats, as some are semi-structured and unstructured too. Managing such data is very difficult, therefore we have some tools for data management such as Flume, Sqoop, and Storm, which are mentioned as follows:

- **Apache Flume**: Apache Flume is a widely used tool for efficiently collecting, aggregating, and moving large amounts of log data from many different sources to a centralized data store. Flume is a distributed, reliable, and available system. It performs well if a source is streaming, for example, log files.

- **Apache Sqoop**: Sqoop can be used to manage data between Hadoop and relational databases, enterprise data warehouses, and NoSQL systems. Sqoop has different connectors with respective data stores and using these connectors, Sqoop can import and export data in MapReduce, and can import and export data in parallel mode. Sqoop is also fault tolerant.

- **Apache Storm**: Apache Storm provides a real-time, scalable, and distributed solution for streaming data. Storm enables data-driven and automated activities. Apache Storm can be used with any programming language and it guarantees that data streams are processed without data loss. Storm is datatype-agnostic, it processes data streams of any data type.

Service programming

Programming in a distributed environment is complex and care has to be taken, otherwise it can become inefficient. To develop properly distributed applications in Hadoop, we have some service programming tools which provide utilities that take care of the distribution and resource management aspect. The tools that we will be discussing are as follows:

- Apache YARN
- Apache Zookeeper

Apache YARN

Yet another Resource Negotiator (YARN) has been a revolution in the major release of Hadoop 2.*x* version. YARN provides resource management and should be utilized as a common platform for integrating different tools and utilities in a Hadoop cluster and managing them. YARN is a resource manager that was created by separating the processing engine and resource management capabilities of MapReduce. It also provides the platform for processing frameworks other than MapReduce such as, Storm, Spark, and so on. YARN has built-in support for multi-tenancy to share cluster resource. YARN is responsible for managing and monitoring workloads and managing high-availability features of Hadoop.

YARN has improved capabilities, so that it can also be tuned for streaming and real-time analysis, which is a huge benefit and need in some scenarios. YARN is also backward compatible for existing MapReduce apps.

Some applications powered by YARN are as follows:

- Apache Hadoop MapReduce
- Apache Spark
- Apache Storm
- Apache Tez
- Apache S4

Apache Zookeeper

ZooKeeper is a distributed, open source coordination service for distributed applications. ZooKeeper exposes a simple set of primitives that distributed applications can use for synchronization, configuration, maintenance, grouping and naming resources for achieving co-ordination, high availability, and synchronization. ZooKeeper runs in Java and has bindings for both Java and C.

HBase, Solr, Kata, Neo4j, and so on, are some tools which use Zookeeper to coordinate activities.

Scheduling

The Hadoop system can have multiple jobs and these have to be scheduled many times. Hadoop jobs' scheduling is complex and difficult to create, manage, and monitor. We can use a system such as Oozie to coordinate and monitor Hadoop jobs efficiently, as mentioned next:

- **Apache Oozie**: Oozie is a workflow and coordination service processing system that lets the users manage multiple jobs as well as chain of jobs written in MapReduce, Pig, and Hive, also java programs and shell sripts too, and can link them to one another. Oozie is an extensible, scalable, and data-aware service. Oozie can be used to set rules for beginning and ending a workflow and it can also detect the completion of tasks.

Data analytics and machine learning

In Hadoop, and for general big data, analytics is the key interest area, as Hadoop is a powerful tool to process complex programs and algorithms to improve the process and business. Data analytics can identify deep insights and can help to optimize the process and stay ahead in the competition. Due to the powerful processing nature of Hadoop, machine learning has been in focus and a lot of development in the algorithms and techniques have been adapted for Hadoop. Machine learning techniques are also used in predictive analytics. Data analytics and machine learning is needed by competitive organizations to stay ahead in the competition and by some researchers, especially in life sciences, to process genes and medical records' patterns to generate much important and useful insights and details that are quite necessary in the medical field. This is also needed by researchers in the field of robotics to provide intelligence to machines for performing and optimizing a task. RHadoop is a data analytics statistical language integrated with Hadoop. Mahout is an open source machine learning API used in Hadoop.

- **Apache Mahout**: Mahout is a scalable machine learning API, which has a lot of implemented machine learning libraries. Mahout is an isolated project which can be used as a pure machine learning library, but the power of Mahout enhances when it is integrated with Hadoop. Some of the algorithms which are popularly used in Mahout are as follows;

  - Recommendation
  - Clustering
  - Classification

System management

Deploying, provisioning, managing, and monitoring a Hadoop cluster requires expert scripting knowledge and usually takes a good amount of effort and time manually, but is repetitive. For performing such activities in Hadoop, we can use tools such as Ambari.

Apache Ambari

Ambari can be used by application developers and system integrators for managing most of the administration activities in a Hadoop cluster. Ambari is an open source framework in the Hadoop ecosystem, which can be used for installing, provisioning, deployment, managing, and monitoring a Hadoop cluster. Ambari's main motive is to hide the complexity of the Hadoop cluster management and to provide a very easy and intuitive web UI. One key feature of Ambari is that it provides RESTful APIs, which can be used to integrate with other external tools for better management.

Summary

In this chapter, we explored the different layers, and some components which can perform the layer functionality in the Hadoop ecosystem, and their usage.

We discussed the Hadoop system on a very high level, and we will be discussing the Hadoop architecture in depth in *Chapter 3, Pillars of Hadoop – HDFS, MapReduce, and YARN*.

3
Pillars of Hadoop – HDFS, MapReduce, and YARN

We discussed in the last two chapters about big data, Hadoop, and the Hadoop ecosystem. Now, let's discuss more technical aspects about **Hadoop Architecture**. Hadoop Architecture is extremely flexible, scalable, and fault tolerant. The key to the success of Hadoop is its architecture that allows the data to be loaded as it is and stored in a distributed way, which has no data loss and no preprocessing is required.

We know that Hadoop is distributed computing and a parallel processing environment. Hadoop architecture can be divided in two parts: storage and processing. Storage in Hadoop is handled by **Hadoop Distributed File System (HDFS)**, **and processing is handled by MapReduce**, as shown in the following image:

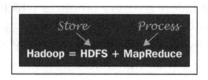

In this chapter, we will cover the basics of HDFS concept, Architecture, some key features, how Read and Write process happens, and some examples. MapReduce is the heart of Hadoop, and we will cover the Architecture, Serialization Data Types, MapReduce Steps or process, various file formats, and an example to write MapReduce programs. After this, we will come to YARN, which is most promising in Hadoop, and many applications have already adopted YARN, which has elevated Hadoop's capability.

HDFS

HDFS is the default storage filesystem in Hadoop, which is distributed, considerably simple in design and extremely scalable, flexible, and with high fault tolerance capability. HDFS architecture has a master-slave pattern due to which the slave nodes can be better managed and utilized. HDFS can even run on commodity hardware, and the architecture accepts that some nodes can be down and still data has to be recovered and processed. HDFS has self-healing processes and speculative execution, which make the system fault tolerant, and is flexible to add/remove nodes and increases the scalability with reliability. HDFS is designed to be best suited for MapReduce programming. One key assumption in HDFS is *Moving Computation is Cheaper than Moving Data.*

Features of HDFS

The important features of HDFS are as follows:

- **Scalability**: HDFS is scalable to petabytes or even more. HDFS is flexible enough to add or remove nodes, which can achieve scalability.

- **Reliability and fault tolerance**: HDFS replicates the data to a configurable parameter, which gives flexibility of getting high reliability and increases the fault tolerance of a system, as data will be stored in multiple nodes, and even if a few nodes are down, data can be accessed from other available nodes.

- **Data Coherency**: HDFS has the **WORM (write once, read many)** model, which simplifies the data coherency and gives high throughput.

- **Hardware failure recovery**: HDFS assumes some nodes in the cluster can fail and has a good failure recovery processes which allows HDFS to run even in commodity hardwares. HDFS has failover processes which can recover the data and handle hardware failure recovery.

- **Portability**: HDFS is portable on different hardwares and softwares.

- **Computation closer to data**: HDFS moves the computation process toward data instead of pulling data out for computation, which is much faster, as data is distributed and ideal for the MapReduce process.

HDFS architecture

HDFS is managed by the daemon processes which are as follows:

- **NameNode**: Master process

- **DataNode**: Slave process
- **Checkpoint NameNode or Secondary NameNode**: Checkpoint process
- **BackupNode**: Backup NameNode

The HDFS architecture is shown in the following screenshot:

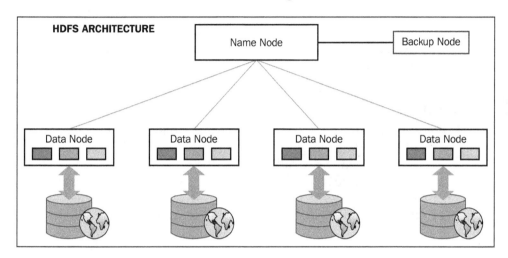

NameNode

NameNode is the master process daemon server in HDFS that coordinates all the operations related to storage in Hadoop, including the read and writes in HDFS. NameNode manages the filesystem namespace. NameNode holds the metadata above all the file blocks, and in which all nodes of data blocks are present in the cluster. NameNode doesn't store any data. NameNode caches the data and stores metadata in RAM for faster access, hence it requires a system with high RAM, otherwise NameNode can become a bottleneck in the cluster processing.

NameNode is a very critical process in HDFS and is a single point of failure, but HDFS can be configured as HDFS HA (high availability), which allows two NameNodes, only one of them can be active at a point of time and the other will be in standby. Standby NameNode will be getting the updates and the DataNode status, which makes Standby NameNode ready to take over and recover, if the active node of NameNode fails.

NameNode maintains the following two metadata files:

- **Fsimage file**: This holds the entire filesystem namespace, including the mapping of blocks to files and filesystem properties
- **Editlog file**: This holds every change that occurs to the filesystem metadata

When NameNode starts up, it reads `FsImage` and `EditLog` files from disk, merges all the transactions present in the `EditLog` to the `FsImage`, and flushes out this new version into a new `FsImage` on disk. It can then truncate the old `EditLog` because its transactions have been applied to the persistent `FsImage`.

DataNode

DataNode holds the actual data in HDFS and is also responsible for creating, deleting, and replicating data blocks, as assigned by NameNode. DataNode sends messages to NameNode, which are called as heartbeat in a periodic interval. If a DataNode fails to send the heartbeat message, then NameNode will mark it as a dead node. If the file data present in the DataNode becomes less than the replication factor, then NameNode replicates the file data to other DataNodes.

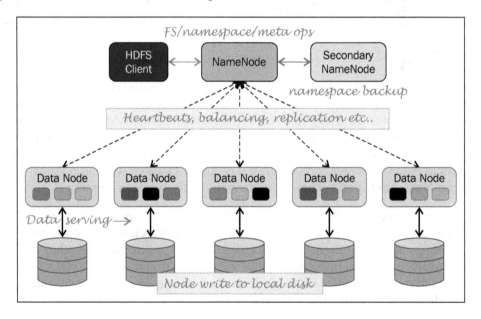

Image source: `http://yoyoclouds.files.wordpress.com/2011/12/hadoop_arch.png`.

Checkpoint NameNode or Secondary NameNode

Checkpoint NameNode , earlier known as Secondary NameNode, is a node that has frequent data check points of `FsImage` and `EditLog` files merged and available for NameNode in case of any NameNode failure. Checkpoint NameNode collects and stores the latest checkpoint. After storing, it merges the changes in the metadata to make it available for NameNode. Checkpoint NameNode usually has to be a separate node, and it requires a similar configuration machine as for NameNode, as memory requirement is the same as NameNode.

BackupNode

BackupNode is similar to Checkpoint NameNode, but it keeps the updated copy of `FsImage` in RAM memory and is always synchronized with NameNode. BackupNode has the same RAM requirement as NameNode. In high availability, BackupNode can be configured as Hot standby Node, and Zookeeper coordinates to make BackupNode as a failover NameNode.

Data storage in HDFS

In HDFS, files are divided in blocks, are stored in multiple DataNodes, and their metadata is stored in NameNode. For understanding how HDFS works, we need to understand some parameters and why it is used. The parameters are as follows:

- **Block**: Files are divided in multiple blocks. Blocks are configurable parameters in HDFS, where we can set the value, and files will be divided in block size: the default block size is 64 MB in the version prior to 2.2.0 and 128 MB since Hadoop 2.2.0 version. Block size is high to minimize the cost of disk seek time (which is slower), leverage transfer rate (which can be high), and reduce the metadata size in NameNode for a file.

- **Replication**: Each block of files divided earlier is stored in multiple DataNodes, and we can configure the number of replication factors. The default value is 3. The replication factor is the key to achieve fault tolerance. The higher the number of the replication factor, the system will be highly fault tolerant and will occupy that many numbers of time the file is saved, and also increase the metadata in NameNode. We have to balance the replication factor, not too high and not too low.

Read pipeline

The HDFS read process can be depicted in the following image:

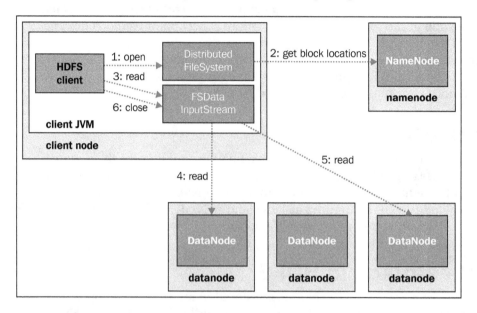

The HDFS read process involves the following six steps:

1. The client using a **Distributed FileSystem** object of Hadoop client API calls open() which initiate the read request.

2. **Distributed FileSystem** connects with **NameNode**. **NameNode** identifies the block locations of the file to be read and in which **DataNodes** the block is located. **NameNode** then sends the list of **DataNodes** in order of nearest DataNodes from the client.

3. **Distributed FileSystem** then creates **FSDataInputStream** objects, which, in turn, wrap a **DFSInputStream**, which can connect to the **DataNodes** selected and get the block, and return to the client. The client initiates the transfer by calling the read() of **FSDataInputStream**.

4. **FSDataInputStream** repeatedly calls the read() method to get the block data.

5. When the end of the block is reached, **DFSInputStream** closes the connection from the DataNode and identifies the best DataNode for the next block.

6. When the client has finished reading, it will call close() on **FSDataInputStream** to close the connection.

Write pipeline

The HDFS write pipeline process flow is summarized in the following image:

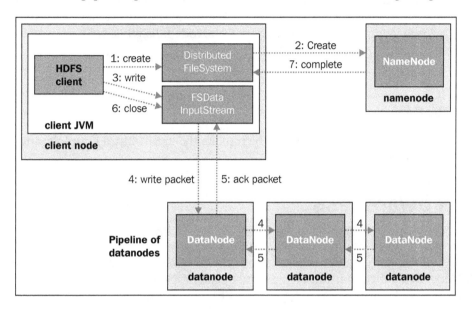

The HDFS write pipeline process flow is described in the following seven steps:

1. The client, using a **Distributed FileSystem** object of Hadoop client API, calls create(), which initiates the write request.

2. **Distributed FileSystem** connects with **NameNode**. **NameNode** initiates a new file creation, and creates a new record in metadata and initiates an output stream of type **FSDataOutputStream**, which wraps **DFSOutputStream** and returns it to the client. Before initiating the file creation, **NameNode** checks if a file already exists and whether the client has permissions to create a new file and if any of the condition is true then an IOException is thrown to the client.

3. The client uses the **FSDataOutputStream** object to write the data and calls the write() method. The **FSDataOutputStream** object, which is DFSOutputStream, handles the communication with the DataNodes and **NameNode**.

4. DFSOutputStream splits files to blocks and coordinates with **NameNode** to identify the **DataNode** and the replica DataNodes. The number of the replication factor will be the number of DataNodes identified. Data will be sent to a **DataNode** in packets, and that **DataNode** will send the same packet to the second **DataNode**, the second **DataNode** will send it to the third, and so on, until the number of DataNodes is identified.

5. When all the packets are received and written, DataNodes send an acknowledgement packet to the sender **DataNode**, to the client. DFSOutputStream maintains a queue internally to check if the packets are successfully written by **DataNode**. DFSOutputStream also handles if the acknowledgment is not received or **DataNode** fails while writing.

6. If all the packets have been successfully written, then the client closes the stream.

7. If the process is completed, then the **Distributed FileSystem** object notifies the **NameNode** of the status.

HDFS has some important concepts which make the architecture fault tolerant and highly available.

Rack awareness

HDFS is fault tolerant, which can be enhanced by configuring rack awareness across the nodes. In a large Hadoop cluster system, DataNodes will be spanned across multiple racks, which can be configured in HDFS to identify rack information of a DataNode. In a simplest form, HDFS can be made rack aware by using a script that can return a rack address for an IP address of nodes. To set the rack mapping script, specify the key `topology.script.file.name` in `conf/hadoop-site.xml`, it must be an executable script or program, which should provide a command to run to return a rack ID.

Rack IDs in Hadoop are hierarchical and look like path names. By default, every node has a rack ID of/default-rack. You can set rack IDs for nodes to any arbitrary path, for example, `/foo/bar-rack`. Path elements further to the left are higher up the tree. Thus, a reasonable structure for a large installation may be `/top-switch-name/rack-name`. The Hadoop rack IDs will be used to find near and far nodes for replica placement.

Advantages of rack awareness in HDFS

Rack awareness can be used to prevent losing data when an entire rack fails and to identify a nearest node where a block is present when reading a file. For efficient rack awareness, a node cannot have two copies of the same block, and in a rack, a block can be present in a maximum of two nodes. The number of racks used for block replication should be always less than the total number of block replicas.

Consider the following scenarios:

- **Writing a block**: When a new block is created, the first replica is placed on the local node, the second one is placed at a different rack, and the third one is placed on a different node at the local rack

- **Reading a block**: For a read request, as in the case of a normal read process, NameNode sends the list of DataNodes in order of DataNodes that are closer from the client and hence gives preference to the DataNodes of the same rack

To verify if a data block is corrupt, HDFS does block scanning. Every DataNode checks the block present in it and verifies with the stored checksum, which is generated during the block creation. Checksum is also verified after an HDFS client reads a block and DataNode gets intimated with the result. Block Scanner is scheduled for three weeks and can also be configured.

In case block corruption is identified, NameNode is informed, and NameNode marks the block in the DataNode as corrupt and initiates a replication of the block, and once a good copy is created and verified with checksum, the block from that DataNode is deleted.

HDFS federation

We have already discussed that NameNode is tightly coupled with DataNodes and is a **SPOF (Single Point of Failure)** in Hadoop 1.*x*. Let's try to understand the limitations of HDFS 1.0 to understand the necessity of HDFS Federation.

Limitations of HDFS 1.0

The following are the limitations:

- **Limitation to number of files**: Even though HDFS can have hundreds and thousands of nodes, as NameNode keeps the metadata in memory, the number of files that can be stored gets limited, depending upon the map heap memory allocated to the NameNode. The limitation arises because of a single NameNode.

- **Single namespace**: Due to a single namespace, the NameNode cannot delegate any workload and can be a bottleneck.

- **SPOF**: NameNode is a single point of failure as it is critical, and too much workload can be there with NameNode.

- **Cannot run non MapReduce applications**: HDFS is only designed to run applications that are MapReduce process or applications that are based on the MapReduce framework.

NameNode has single namespace and is tightly coupled with DataNodes, as all the requests have to coordinate with NameNode to get the blocks' location, and due to which it can become a bottleneck. NameNode has to be highly available or else the request will not be serviced. HDFS Federation is a feature that enables Hadoop to have independent multiple namespaces that overcome the limitations that we discussed. Lets have a look at the following image:

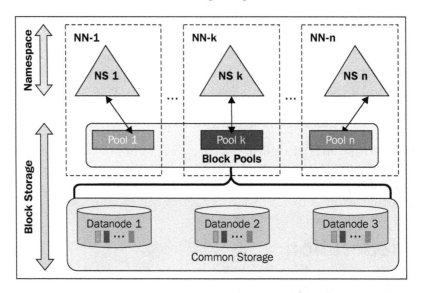

With multiple independent namespace hierarchy, the responsibility of NameNode is shared across multiple namespaces, which are federated but share the DataNodes of the cluster. Due to the Federation of NameNode, some requests can get load balanced among the NameNodes. Federated NameNodes work in multi-tenant architecture to provide isolation.

The benefit of HDFS federation

Read and write process is faster due to multiple NameNodes by avoiding bottleneck in case of a single NameNode process.

Horizontal scalability is achieved by HDFS Federation, which has a huge advantage of being a highly available process and can also act as a load balancer.

HDFS ports

In the Hadoop ecosystem, components have different ports and communication happens by their respective ports. Usually, the port number will be hard to remember.

The default HDFS web UI ports are as summarized in Hortonworks docs at
`http://docs.hortonworks.com/HDPDocuments/HDP1/HDP-1.2.0/bk_reference/`
`content/reference_chap2_1.html`.

Service	Servers	Default Ports Used	Protocol	Description	Need End User Access?	Configuration Parameters
NameNode WebUI	Master Nodes (NameNode and any back-up NameNodes)	50070	http	Web UI to look at current status of HDFS, explore filesystem	Yes (Typically admins, Dev/ Support teams)	dfs.http.address
		50470	https	Secure http service		dfs.https. address
NameNode metadata service	Master Nodes (NameNode and any back-up NameNodes)	8020/9000	IPC	Filesystem metadata operations	Yes (All clients who directly need to interact with HDFS)	Embedded in URI specified by fs.default. name
DataNode	All Slave Nodes	50075	http	DataNode WebUI to access the status, logs etc.	Yes (Typically admins, Dev/ Support teams)	dfs.datanode. http.address
		50475	https	Secure http service		dfs.datanode. https.address
		50010		Data transfer		dfs.datanode. address
		50020	IPC	Metadata operations	No	dfs.datanode. ipc.address
Checkpoint NameNode or Secondary NameNode	Secondary NameNode and any backup Secondary NameNode	50090	http	Checkpoint for NameNode metadata	No	dfs.secondary. http.address

HDFS commands

The Hadoop command line environment is Linux-like. The Hadoop filesystem (fs) provides various shell commands to perform file operations such as copying file, viewing the contents of the file, changing ownership of files, changing permissions, creating directories, and so on.

The syntax of Hadoop fs shell command is as follows:

```
hadoop fs <args>
```

1. Create a directory in HDFS at the given path(s):
   - Usage:
     ```
     hadoop fs -mkdir <paths>
     ```
   - Example:
     ```
     hadoop fs -mkdir /user/shiva/dir1 /user/shiva/dir2
     ```

2. List the contents of a directory:
   - Usage:
     ```
     hadoop fs -ls <args>
     ```
   - Example:
     ```
     hadoop fs -ls /user/shiva
     ```

3. Put and Get a file in HDFS:
   - Usage(Put):
     ```
     hadoop fs -put <localsrc> ... <HDFS_dest_Path>
     ```
   - Example:
     ```
     hadoop fs -put /home/shiva/Samplefile.txt  /user/shiva/dir3/
     ```
   - Usage(Get):
     ```
     hadoop fs -get <hdfs_src> <localdst>
     ```
   - Example:
     ```
     hadoop fs -get /user/shiva/dir3/Samplefile.txt /home/
     ```

4. See contents of a file:
   - Usage:
     ```
     hadoop fs -cat <path[filename]>
     ```

  ° Example:

```
hadoop fs -cat /user/shiva/dir1/abc.txt
```

5. Copy a file from source to destination:

  ° Usage:

```
hadoop fs -cp <source> <dest>
```

  ° Example:

```
hadoop fs -cp /user/shiva/dir1/abc.txt /user/shiva/dir2
```

6. Copy a file from/To Local filesystem to HDFS:

  ° Usage of copyFromLocal:

```
hadoop fs -copyFromLocal <localsrc> URI
```

  ° Example:

```
hadoop fs -copyFromLocal /home/shiva/abc.txt
/user/shiva/abc.txt
```

  ° Usage of copyToLocal

```
hadoop fs -copyToLocal [-ignorecrc] [-crc] URI <localdst>
```

7. Move file from source to destination:

  ° Usage:

```
hadoop fs -mv <src> <dest>
```

  ° Example:

```
hadoop fs -mv /user/shiva/dir1/abc.txt /user/shiva/dir2
```

8. Remove a file or directory in HDFS:

  ° Usage:

```
hadoop fs -rm <arg>
```

  ° Example:

```
hadoop fs -rm /user/shiva/dir1/abc.txt
```

  ° Usage of the recursive version of delete:

```
hadoop fs -rmr <arg>
```

  ° Example:

```
hadoop fs -rmr /user/shiva/
```

9. Display the last few lines of a file:

   ° Usage:

   ```
   hadoop fs -tail <path[filename]>
   ```

   ° Example:

   ```
   hadoop fs -tail /user/shiva/dir1/abc.txt
   ```

MapReduce

MapReduce is a massive parallel processing framework that processes faster, scalable, and fault tolerant data of a distributed environment. Similar to HDFS, Hadoop MapReduce can also be executed even in commodity hardware, and assumes that nodes can fail anytime and still process the job. MapReduce can process a large volume of data in parallel, by dividing a task into independent sub-tasks. MapReduce also has a master-slave architecture.

The input and output, even the intermediary output in a MapReduce job, are in the form of <Key, Value> pair. Key and Value have to be serializable and do not use the Java serialization package, but have an interface, which has to be implemented, and which can be efficiently serialized, as the data process has to move from one node to another. Key has to be a class that implements a WritableComparable interface, which is necessary for sorting the key, and Value has to be a class that implements a Writable interface.

The MapReduce architecture

MapReduce architecture has the following two daemon processes:

- JobTracker: Master process
- TaskTracker : Slave process

JobTracker

JobTracker is the master coordinator daemon process that is responsible for coordinating and completing a MapReduce job in Hadoop. The primary functions of JobTracker are resource management, tracking resource availability, and task process cycle. JobTracker identifies the TaskTracker to perform certain tasks and monitors the progress and status of a task. JobTracker is a single point of failure for the MapReduce process.

TaskTracker

TaskTracker is the slave daemon process that performs a task assigned by JobTracker. TaskTracker sends heartbeat messages to JobTracker periodically to notify about the free slots and sends the status to JobTracker about the task and checks if any task has to be performed.

Serialization data types

Serialization in MapReduce is extremely important as the data and intermediate data have to move from one TaskTracker to another on a very large scale. Java serialization is not optimized, as even for a smaller value, the object serializer will have higher size, which could be a bottleneck in Hadoop's performance as Hadoop processing requires a lot of data transfer. Hence, Hadoop doesn't use the Java serialization package and uses the Writable interface.

For serialization, Hadoop uses the following two interfaces:

- Writable interface (for values)
- WritableComparable interface (for key)

The Writable interface

The Writable interface is used for values for serialization and deserialization. Some of the classes that implement the Writable interface are `ArrayWritable`, `BooleanWritable`, `ByteWritable`, `DoubleWritable`, `FloatWritable`, `IntWritable`, `LongWritable`, `MapWritable`, `NullWritable`, `ObjectWritable`, `ShortWritable`, `TupleWritable`, `VIntWritable`, and `VLongWritable`.

We can create our own custom Writable class that can be used in MapReduce. For creating a class, we have to implement the Writable class and implement the following two methods:

- `void write (DataOutput out)`: This serializes the object
- `void readFields (DataInput in)`: This reads the input stream and converts it to an object

WritableComparable interface

WritableComparable is used for keys, which is inherited from the Writable interface and implements a comparable interface to provide comparison of value Objects. Some of the implementations are `BooleanWritable`, `BytesWritable`, `ByteWritable`, `DoubleWritable`, `FloatWritable`, `IntWritable`, `LongWritable`, `NullWritable`, `ShortWritable`, `Text`, `VIntWritable`, and `VLongWritable`.

We can create our own custom WritableComparable class that can be used in MapReduce. For creating a class, we have to implement WritableComparable class and implement the following three methods:

- `void write (DataPutput out)`: This serializes the object
- `void readFields (DataInput in)`: This reads the input stream and converts it to an object
- `Int compareTo (Object obj)`: Compare the values required to sort the key

The MapReduce example

MapReduce is tricky to understand initially, so we will try to understand it with a simple example. Let's assume we have a file that has some words and the file is divided into blocks in HDFS, and we have to count the number of occurrences of a word in the file. We will go step by step to achieve the result using MapReduce functionality. The whole process is illustrated in the following diagram:

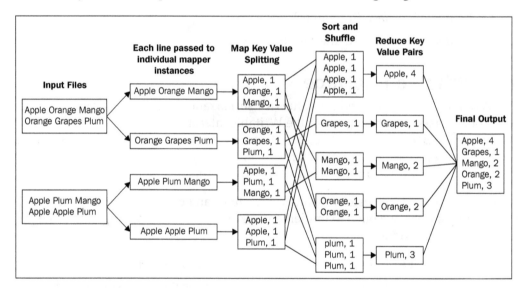

Downloading the example code

You can download the example code files from your account at `http://www.packtpub.com` for all the Packt Publishing books you have purchased. If you purchased this book elsewhere, you can visit `http://www.packtpub.com/support` and register to have the files e-mailed directly to you.

The following is the description of the preceding image:

1. Each block will be processed. Each line in the block will be sent as an input to the process. This process is called as **Mapper**.

    Mapper parses the line, gets a word and sets `<<word>, 1>` for each word. In this example, the output of Mapper for a line **Apple Orange Mango** will be <Apple, 1>, <Orange, 1>, and <Mango, 1>. All Mappers will have key as word and value as 1.

2. The next phase is where the output of Mapper, which has the same key will be consolidated. So key with Apple, Orange, Mango, and others will be consolidated, and values will be appended as a list, in this case

    `<Apple, List<1, 1, 1, 1>>, <Grapes, List<1>>, <Mango, List<1, 1>>,` and so on.

    The key produced by Mappers will be compared and sorted. This step is called shuffle and sort. The key and list of values will be sent to the next step in the sorted sequence of the key.

3. The next phase will get `<key, List<>>` as input, and will just count the number of 1s in the list and will set the count value as output. This step is called as **Reducer**, for example, the output for the certain steps are given as follows:

    - `<Apple, List<1, 1, 1, 1>>` will be `<Apple, 4>`
    - `<Grapes, List<1>>` will be `< Grapes, 1>`
    - `<Mango, List<1, 1>>` will be `<Mango, 2>`

4. The Reducer output will be consolidated to a file and will be saved in HDFS as the final output.

The MapReduce process

MapReduce frameworks have multiple steps and processes or tasks. For programmers, MapReduce abstracts most of them and, in many of the cases, only have to care about two processes; Map and Reduce and to coordinate the process, a Driver class program has to be written. In the Driver class, we can set various parameters to run a MapReduce job from input, Mapper class, Reducer class, output, and other parameters required for a MapReduce job to execute.

MapReduce jobs are complex and involve multiple steps; some steps are performed by Hadoop with default behavior and can be overridden if needed. The following are the mandatory steps performed in MapReduce in sequence:

1. Mapper
2. Shuffle and sorting
3. Reducer

The preceding process is explained in the following figure:

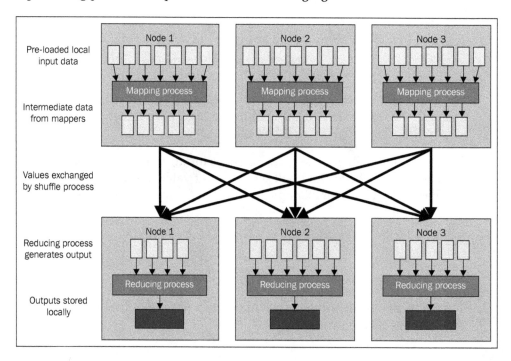

Image source: Hadoop Tutorial from Yahoo!

Mapper

In MapReduce, the parallelism will be achieved by Mapper, where the Mapper function will be present in TaskTracker, which will process a Mapper. Mapper code should have a logic, which can be independent of other block data. Mapper logic should leverage all the parallel steps possible in the algorithm. Input to Mapper is set in the Driver program of a particular InputFormat type and file(s) on which the Mapper process has to run. The output of Mapper will be a map `<key, value>`, key and `value` set in Mapper output is not saved in HDFS, but an intermediate file is created in the OS space path and that file is read and shuffle and sorting takes place.

Shuffle and sorting

Shuffle and sort are intermediate steps in MapReduce between Mapper and Reducer, which is handled by Hadoop and can be overridden if required. The Shuffle process aggregates all the Mapper output by grouping key values of the Mapper output and the value will be appended in a list of values. So, the Shuffle output format will be a map `<key, List<list of values>>`. The key from the Mapper output will be consolidated and sorted. The Mapper output will be sent to Reducer using the sorted key sequence by default a `HashPartitioner`, which will send the Mapper result in a round robin style of the sequence of number of reducers with the sorted sequence.

Reducer

In MapReduce, Reducer is the aggregator process where data after shuffle and sort, is sent to Reducer where we have `<key, List<list of values >>`, and Reducer will process on the list of values. Each key could be sent to a different Reducer. Reducer can set the value, and that will be consolidated in the final output of a MapReduce job and the value will be saved in HDFS as the final output.

Speculative execution

As we discussed, MapReduce jobs are broken into multiple Mapper and Reducer processes, and some intermediate tasks, so that a job can produce hundreds or thousands of tasks, and some tasks or nodes can take a long time to complete a task. Hadoop monitors and detects when a task is running slower than expectation, and if the node has a history of performing the task slower, then it starts the same task in another node as a backup, and this is called as speculative execution of tasks. Hadoop doesn't try to fix or diagnose the node or process, since the process is not giving an error, but it is slow, and slowness can occur because of hardware degradation, software misconfiguration, network congestion, and so on. For speculative execution, JobTracker monitors the tasks after all the tasks have been initiated and identifies slow performing tasks monitoring other running tasks. Once the slow performing task has been marked, JobTracker initiates the task in a different node and takes the result of the task that completes first and kills the other tasks and makes a note of the situation. If a node is consistently lagging behind, then JobTracker gives less preference to that node.

Speculative execution can be enabled or disabled, and by default it is turned on, as it is a useful process. Speculative execution has to monitor every task in some cases can affect the performance and resources. Speculation Execution is not advised in jobs where a task especially reducer can get millions of values due to skewness in data on a specific reducer which will take longer time than other tasks and starting another task will not help. Another case could be of a Sqoop process where a task imports the data and if it takes more than the usual time it can start same task in another node and will import the same data which will result in duplicate records.

FileFormats

FileFormats controls the input and output in MapReduce programs. Some FileFormats can be considered as data structures. Hadoop provides some implemented FileFormats, and we can write our own custom FileFormats too. We will have a look at them in the upcoming section.

InputFormats

The Mapper process steps provide the parallelism, and for faster processing, Mapper has to be designed optimally. For performing the data independently, Input data to Mapper is split into chunks called as InputSplit. InputSplit can be considered as a part of input data, where data can be processed independently. A Mapper processes on an InputSplit of data. Input to a MapReduce job has to be defined as a class implementing the InputFormat interface and RecordReader is sometimes necessary to read data between splits to identify independent chunks of data from the input data file.

Hadoop already has different types of InputFormat for the interpretation of various types of input data and reading the data from the input file. InputFormat splits the input file in fragments that are input to the map task. Examples of InputFormat classes implemented are as follows:

- TextInputFormat is used to read text files line by line
- SequenceFileInputFormat is used to read binary file formats
- DBInputFormat subclass is a class that can be used to read data from a SQL database
- CombineFileInputFormat is the abstract subclass of the FileInputFormat class that can be used to combine multiple files into a single split

We can create our own custom InputFormat classes by implementing the InputFormat interface or extending any class that implements InputFormats. Extending the class is preferred as many of the functions written are reusable, which helps in maintainability and reusability of a code. The class would have to override the following two functions:

- `public RecordReader createRecordReader(InputSplit split, TaskAttemptContext context) throws IOException, InterruptedException`
- `protected boolean isSplitable(JobContext context, Path file)`

RecordReader

InputFormat splits the data, but splits do not always end neatly at the end of a line. The RecordReader can allow data even if the line crosses the end of the split or else chances are of missing records that might have crossed the InputSplit boundaries.

The following figure explains the concept of RecordReader where the block size is 128 MB and the split size is 50 MB:

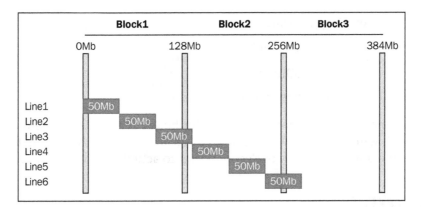

We can see that there are overlaps of data split between different blocks. Splits 1 and 2 can be read from **Block1**, but for split 3, RecordReader has to read locally from 101 MB to 128 MB and from 129 MB to 150 MB has to be read remotely from **Block 2** and the merged data will be sent as an input to Mapper.

OutputFormats

OutputFormat implementation classes are responsible for writing the output and results of a MapReduce job, it gives control of how you want to write the record efficiently to optimize the result, and can be used to write the format of the data for inter-operability with other systems. The default OutputFormat is TextOutputFormat (we used this as an output to our WordCount example), which is key–value pair line separated and tab delimited. TextOutputFormat can be used in many use cases, but not in an optimized or efficient way, as it can waste space and can make the output size larger and increase the resource utilization. Hence, we can reuse some OutputFormats provided by Hadoop or can even write custom OutputFormats.

Some available OutputFormats that are widely used, are as follows:

1. FileOutputFormat (implements the interface OutputFormat) base class for all OutputFormats

    ° MapFileOutputFormat

    ° SequenceFileOutputFormat

    SequenceFileAsBinaryOutputFormat

    ° TextOutputFormat

    ° MultipleOutputFormat

    MultipleTextOutputFormat

    MultipleSequenceFileOutputFormat

2. SequenceOutputFormat can be used for binary representation of the object, which it compresses and writes as an output. OutputFormats use the implementation of RecordWriter to actually write the data.

RecordWriter

RecordWriter interface provides more control to write the data as we want. RecordWriter takes the input as key-value pair and can translate the format of the data to write.

RecordWriter is an abstract class, which has two methods to be implemented, as shown in the following:

```
abstract void write(K key, V value)
    Writes a key/value pair.
abstract void close(TaskAttemptContext context)
    Close this RecordWriter to future operations.
```

The default RecordWriter is LineRecordWriter.

Writing a MapReduce program

A MapReduce job class will have the following three mandatory classes or tasks:

*   **Mapper**: In the Mapper class, the actual independent steps are written, which are parallelized to run in independent sub-tasks

*   **Reducer**: In the Reducer class, the aggregation of the Mapper output takes place and the output is written in HDFS

- **Driver**: In the Driver class, we can set various parameters to run a MapReduce job from input, Mapper class, Reducer class, output, and other parameters required for a MapReduce job to execute

We have already seen the logic of a simple WordCount example to illustrate how MapReduce works. Now, we will see how to code it in the Java MapReduce program.

Mapper code

A Mapper class has to extend

```
org.apache.hadoop.mapreduce.Mapper<KEYIN,VALUEIN,KEYOUT,VALUEOUT>.
```

The following is the snippet of the Mapper class code:

```
// And override
public void map(Object key, Text value, Context context)
  throws IOException, InterruptedException
public static class WordCountMapper extends
  Mapper<Object, Text, Text, IntWritable> {

    private final static IntWritable one = new IntWritable(1);
    private Text word = new Text();

    public void map(Object key, Text value, Context context)
      throws IOException, InterruptedException {
      StringTokenizer token = new
        StringTokenizer(value.toString());
      while (token.hasMoreTokens()) {
        word.set(token.nextToken());
        context.write(word, one);
      }
    }
  }
}
```

In a map function, the input value (Apple, Orange, Mango) has to be tokenized, and the tokenized word will be written as Mapper key and value as 1. Note that value 1 is IntWritable.

Reducer code

A Reducer class has to extend

```
org.apache.hadoop.mapreduce.Reducer<KEYIN,VALUEIN,KEYOUT,VALUEOUT>.
```

The following is the code for WordCountReducer:

```
// and override reduce function
protected void reduce(KEYIN key, Iterable<VALUEIN> values,
org.apache.hadoop.mapreduce.Reducer.Context context)
throws IOException, InterruptedException
public static class WordCountReducer
      extends Reducer<Text,IntWritable,Text,IntWritable> {
   private IntWritable count = new IntWritable();

   public void reduce(Text key, Iterable<IntWritable> values,
                     Context context
                     ) throws IOException, InterruptedException {
     int sum = 0;
     for (IntWritable val : values) {
       sum += val.get();
     }
     count.set(sum);
     context.write(key, count);
   }
}
```

Reducer input will be <word, List<1,1,…>> for WordCount Reducer has to sum the list of values and write the value. Reducer output will be the key as word and value as count.

Driver code

Driver code in MapReduce will be mostly boiler plate code with just changes in the parameters, and may need to set some Auxiliary class, as shown in the following:

```
public static void main(String[] args) throws Exception {
   Configuration conf = new Configuration();
   Job job = Job.getInstance(conf, "word count");
   job.setJarByClass(WordCount.class);
   job.setMapperClass(WordCountMapper.class);
   job.setReducerClass(WordCountReducer.class);
   job.setOutputKeyClass(Text.class);
   job.setOutputValueClass(IntWritable.class);
   FileInputFormat.addInputPath(job, new Path(args[0]));
   FileOutputFormat.setOutputPath(job, new Path(args[1]));
   System.exit(job.waitForCompletion(true) ? 0 : 1);
}
```

Driver code has to create an instance of the `Configuration` object, which is used to get an instance of `Job` class. In `Job` class, we can set the following:

- MapperClass
- ReducerClass
- OutputKeyClass
- OutputValueClass
- InputFormat
- OutputFormat
- JarByClass

The whole program of WordCount is as follows:

```
import java.io.IOException;
import java.util.StringTokenizer;

import org.apache.hadoop.conf.Configuration;
import org.apache.hadoop.fs.Path;
import org.apache.hadoop.io.IntWritable;
import org.apache.hadoop.io.Text;
import org.apache.hadoop.mapreduce.Job;
import org.apache.hadoop.mapreduce.Mapper;
import org.apache.hadoop.mapreduce.Reducer;
import org.apache.hadoop.mapreduce.lib.input.FileInputFormat;
import org.apache.hadoop.mapreduce.lib.output.FileOutputFormat;

public class WordCount {

  public static class WordCountMapper
      extends Mapper<Object, Text, Text, IntWritable>{

    private final static IntWritable one = new IntWritable(1);
    private Text word = new Text();

    public void map(Object key, Text value, Context context)
      throws IOException, InterruptedException {
      StringTokenizer token = new
        StringTokenizer(value.toString());
```

```java
      while (token.hasMoreTokens()) {
        word.set(token.nextToken());
        context.write(word, one);
      }
    }
  }

  public static class WordCountReducer extends
    Reducer<Text,IntWritable,Text,IntWritable> {
    private IntWritable count = new IntWritable();

    public void reduce(Text key, Iterable<IntWritable> values,
      Context context) throws IOException, InterruptedException {
      int sum = 0;
      for (IntWritable val : values) {
        sum += val.get();
      }
      count.set(sum);
      context.write(key, count);
    }
  }

  public static void main(String[] args) throws Exception {
    Configuration conf = new Configuration();
    Job job = Job.getInstance(conf, "word count");
    job.setJarByClass(WordCount.class);
    job.setMapperClass(WordCountMapper.class);
    job.setReducerClass(WordCountReducer.class);
    job.setOutputKeyClass(Text.class);
    job.setOutputValueClass(IntWritable.class);
    FileInputFormat.addInputPath(job, new Path(args[0]));
    FileOutputFormat.setOutputPath(job, new Path(args[1]));
    System.exit(job.waitForCompletion(true) ? 0 : 1);
  }
}
```

Compile `WordCount.java` and create a jar.

Run the application:

```
$ bin/hadoop jar wc.jar WordCount /input /user/shiva/wordcount/output
```

Output:

```
$ bin/hdfs dfs -cat /user/shiva/wordcount/output/part-r-00000
```

Auxiliary steps

Along with Mapper, shuffle and sort, and Reducer, there are other auxiliary steps in MapReduce that can be set, or a default implementation can be overridden to process the MapReduce job. The following are some processes which we will discuss:

- Combiner
- Partitioner

The preceding points are discussed in the following figure:

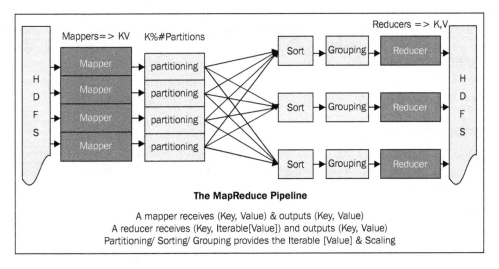

The MapReduce Pipeline

A mapper receives (Key, Value) & outputs (Key, Value)
A reducer receives (Key, Iterable[Value]) and outputs (Key, Value)
Partitioning/ Sorting/ Grouping provides the Iterable [Value] & Scaling

Combiner

Combiners are node-local reducers. Combiners are used to reduce the number of key values set by Mapper, and we can reduce the number of data sent for shuffling. Many programs would have Reducer as the Combiner class and can have a different implementation from Reducer if needed, The combiner is specified for a job using `job.setCombinerClass(CombinerClassName)`.

Combiner should have the same input/output key and value types as the output types of your Mapper. Combiners can only be used on the functions that are commutative (`a.b = b.a`) and associative `{a. (b.c) = (a.b).c}`.

In the WordCount example, we can use a combiner, which can be the same as the Reducer class and will improve the performance of the job.

Combiner will not always be processed by JobTracker. If the data in Mapper spills out then Combiner will surely be called.

Partitioner

Partitioner is responsible for sending specific key-value pairs to specific reducers. `HashPartitioner` is the default Partitioner, which hashes a record's key to determine which partition the record belongs to, in a round robin fashion, according to the number of Reducers, if specified, or the number of partitions is then equal to the number of reduce tasks for the job. Partitioning is sometimes required to control the key-value pairs from Mapper to move to particular Reducers. Partitioning has a direct impact on the overall performance of the job we want to run.

Custom partitioner

Suppose we want to sort the output of the WordCount on the basis of the number of occurrences of tokens. Assume that our job will be handled by two reducers, as shown in the following:

Setting Number of Reducer: We can specify that by using `job.setNumReduceTasks(#NoOfReducucer)`.

If we run our job without using any user defined Partitioner, we will get output like the following:

Count	Word	Count	Word
1	The	2	a
3	Is	4	because
6	As	5	of
Reducer 1		Reducer 2	

This is a partial sort, which is the default behavior of `HashPartitioner`. If we use the correct partitioning function, we can send a count less than, or equal to, 3 to a reducer and higher to another, and we have to set `setNumReduceTasks` as 2. We will get the total order on the number of occurrences.

The output would look like the following:

Count	Word	Count	Word
1	The	4	because
2	A	5	as
3	Is	6	of
Reducer 1		Reducer 2	

Let's look at how can we write a custom `Partitioner` class, as shown in the following:

```
public static class MyPartitioner extends    org.apache.hadoop.
mapreduce.Partitioner<Text,Text>

{
  @Override
  public int getPartition(Text key, Text value, int numPartitions)
  {
   int count =Integer.parseInt(line[1]);
   if(count<=3)
    return 0;
   else
    return 1;
  }
}

And in Driver class
job.setPartitionerClass(MyPartitioner.class);
```

YARN

YARN is **Yet Another Resource Negotiator**, the next generation compute and cluster management technology. YARN provides a platform to build/run multiple distributed applications in Hadoop. YARN was released in the Hadoop 2.0 version in 2012, marking a major change in Hadoop architecture. YARN took around 5 years to develop in an open community.

We discussed JobTracker being a single point of failure for MapReduce, and considering Hadoop is designed to run even in commodity servers, there is a good probability that the JobTracker can fail. JobTracker has two important functions: resource management, and job scheduling and monitoring.

YARN delegates and splits up the responsibility into separate daemons and achieves better performance and fault tolerance. Because of YARN, Hadoop, which could work only as a batch process, can now be designed to process interactive and real-time processing systems. This is a huge advantage as many systems, machines, sensors, and other sources generate huge data continuously streaming and YARN can process this data, as depicted in the following figure:

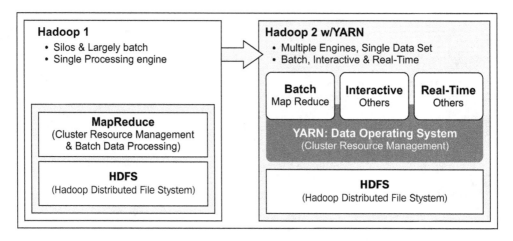

Image source: http://hortonworks.com/labs/yarn/

YARN architecture

YARN architecture is extremely scalable, fault tolerant, and processes data faster as compared to MapReduce 1.*x*. YARN focuses on high availability and utilization of resources in the cluster. YARN architecture has the following three components:

- **ResourceManager (RM)**
- **NodeManager (NM)**
- **ApplicationMaster (AM)**

YARN architecture is illustrated in the following image:

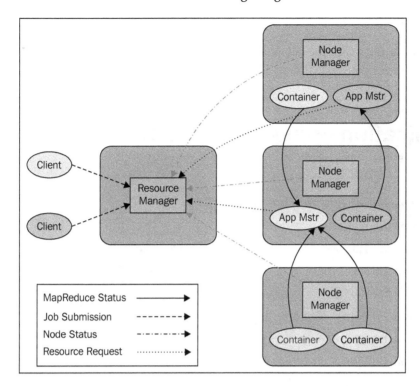

Image source: `http://hadoop.apache.org/docs/current/hadoop-yarn/hadoop-yarn-site/YARN.html`.

ResourceManager

In YARN, ResourceManager is the master process manager responsible for resource management among the applications in the system. ResourceManager has a scheduler, which only allocates the resources to the applications and resource availability which ResourceManager gets from containers that provide information such as memory, disk, CPU, network, and so on.

NodeManager

In YARN, NodeManager is present in all the nodes, which is responsible for containers, authentication, monitoring resource usage, and reports the information to ResourceManager. Similar to TaskTracker, NodeManager sends heartbeats to ResourceManager.

ApplicationMaster

ApplicationMaster is present for each application, responsible for managing each and every instance of applications that run within YARN. ApplicationMaster coordinates with ResourceManager for the negotiation of the resources and coordinates with the NodeManager to monitor the execution and resource consumption of containers, such as resource allocations of CPU, memory, and so on.

Applications powered by YARN

Below are some of the applications that have adapted YARN to leverage its features and achieve high availability:

- **Apache Giraph**: Graph processing
- **Apache Hama**: Advanced Analytics
- **Apache Hadoop MapReduce**: Batch processing
- **Apache Tez**: Interactive/Batch on top of Hive
- **Apache S4**: Stream processing
- **Apache Samza**: Stream processing
- **Apache Storm**: Stream processing
- **Apache Spark**: Realtime Iterative processing
- **Hoya**: Hbase on YARN

Summary

In this chapter, we have discussed HDFS, MapReduce, and YARN in detail.

HDFS is highly scalable, fault tolerant, reliable, and portable, and is designed to work even on commodity hardwares. HDFS architecture has four daemon processes, which are NameNode, DataNode, Checkpoint NameNode, and Backup Node. HDFS has a lot of complex design challenges, which are managed by different techniques such as Replication, Heartbeat, Block concept, Rack Awareness, and Block Scanner, and HDFS Federation makes HDFS highly available and fault tolerant.

Hadoop MapReduce is also highly scalable, fault tolerant, and designed to work even in commodity hardwares. MapReduce architecture has a master JobTracker and multiple worker TaskTracker processes in the Nodes. MapReduce jobs are broken into multistep processes, which are Mapper, Shuffle, Sort, Reducer, and auxiliary Combiner and Partitioner. MapReduce jobs needs a lot of data transfer, for which Hadoop uses Writable and WritableComparable interfaces. MapReduce FileFormats has an InputFormat interface, RecordReader, OutputFormat, and RecordWriter to improve the processing and efficiency.

YARN is a distributed resource manager to manage and run different applications on top of Hadoop, and provides much needed enhancements to the MapReduce framework, that can make Hadoop much more available, scalable, and integrable. YARN Architecture has the following components: ResourceManager, NodeManager, and ApplicationMaster. Many applications are built on top of YARN, which has made Hadoop much more stable and integrable with other applications.

In the next chapter, we will cover Data Access component technologies, which are used in the Hadoop ecosystem, such as Hive and Pig, as it helps to ease the programming model and makes it faster and more maintainable.

Data Access Components – Hive and Pig

4

Hadoop can usually hold terabytes or petabytes of data to process; hence Data Access is an extremely important aspect in any project or product, especially with Hadoop. As we deal with Big Data for processing data, we will have to perform some ad hoc processing to get insights of data and design strategies. Hadoop's basic processing layer is MapReduce, which as we discussed earlier, is a massively parallel processing framework that is scalable, faster, adaptable, and fault tolerant.

We will look at some limitations of MapReduce programming and some programming abstraction layers such as Hive and Pig in detail, which can execute MapReduce using a user friendly language for faster development and management. Hive and Pig are quite useful and handy when it comes to easily do some ad hoc analysis and some not very complex analysis.

Need of a data processing tool on Hadoop

MapReduce is the key to perform processing on Big Data, but it is complex to understand, design, code, and optimize. MapReduce has a high learning curve, which requires good programming skills to master. Usually Big Data users come from different backgrounds such as Programming, Database administrators, scripting, Analyst, Data science, Data Managers, and so on, and not all users can adapt to the programming model of MapReduce. Hence we have different abstractions for the data access components for Hadoop.

The data access components are very useful for developers as they may not need to learn MapReduce programming in detail and can still utilize the MapReduce framework in an interface in which they can be much more comfortable and can help in faster development and better manageability of the code. Abstractions can help ad hoc processing on data quickly and concentrate on the business logic.

The two widely used data access components in the Hadoop ecosystem are:

- Pig
- Hive

Let us discuss each of these in detail with some examples.

Pig

Pig is a component which has the abstraction wrapper of Pig Latin language on top of MapReduce. Pig was developed by Yahoo! around 2006 and was contributed to Apache as an open source project. Pig Latin is a data flow language that is more comfortable for a procedural language developer or user. Pig can help manage the data in a flow which is ideal for the data flow process, ETL (Extract Transform Load), or the ELT (Extract Load Transform) process ad hoc data analysis.

Pig can be used in a much easier way for structured and semi-structured data analysis. Pig was developed based on a philosophy, which is that Pigs can eat anything, live anywhere, can be easily controlled and modified by the user, and it is important to process data quickly.

Pig data types

Pig has a collection of primitive data types, as well as complex data types. Inputs and outputs to Pig's relational operators are specified using these data types:

- **Primitive**: int, long, float, double, chararray, and bytearray
- **Map**: Map is an associative array data type that stores a chararray key and its associated value. The data type of a value in a map can be a complex type. If the type of the value cannot be determined, Pig defaults to the bytearray data type. The key and value association is specified as the # symbol. The key values within a map have to be unique.

  Syntax: `[key#value, key1#value1...]`

- **Tuple**: A tuple data type is a collection of data values. They are of fixed length and ordered. Tuple is similar to a record in a SQL table, without restrictions on the column types. Each data value is called a field. Ordering of values offers the capability to randomly access a value within a tuple.

  Syntax: (value1, value2, value3…)

- **Bag**: A bag data type is a container for tuples and other bags. They are unordered, that is, a tuple or a bag within a bag cannot be accessed randomly. There are no constraints on the structure of the tuples contained in a bag. Duplicate tuples or bags are allowed within a bag.

  Syntax: {(tuple1), (tuple2)…}

Pig allows nesting of complex data structures where you can nest a tuple inside a tuple, a bag, and a Map. Pig Latin statements work with relations, which can be thought of as:

- A relation (similar to, database table) is a bag
- A bag is a collection of tuples
- A tuple (similar to, database row) is an ordered set of fields
- A field is a piece of data

The Pig architecture

The Pig data flow architecture is layered for transforming Pig Latin statements to MapReduce steps. There are three main phases in compiling and executing a Pig script, which are as follows:

- Logical plan
- Physical plan
- MapReduce plan

The logical plan

In the logical plan, the Pig statements are parsed for syntax errors and validation of the input files and input data structures. A logical plan, a DAG (Directed Acyclic Graph) of operators as nodes, and data flow as edges are then prepared. Optimizations based on in-built rules happen at this stage. The logical plan has a one-to-one correspondence with the operators.

The physical plan

A translation of each operator into the physical form of execution happens during this stage. For the MapReduce platform, except for a few, most operators have a one-to-one correspondence with the physical plan. In addition to the logical operators, there are a few physical operators too. They are as follows:

- Local Rearrange (LR)
- Global Rearrange (GR)
- Package (P)

Logical operators like GROUP, COGROUP, or JOIN are translated into a sequence of LR, GR, and P operators. The LR operator corresponds to the shuffle preparation stage, where partitioning happens based on the key. The GR corresponds to the actual shuffle between the Map and Reduce tasks. The P operator is the partitioning operator on the Reduce side.

The MapReduce plan

The final stage of Pig compilation is to compile the physical plan to actual MapReduce jobs. A Reduce task is required wherever a LR, GR, and P sequence is present in the physical plan. The compiler also looks for opportunities to put in Combiners wherever possible. The MapReduce plan for the physical plan in the previous image has two MapReduce jobs, one corresponding to the JOIN and the other to the GROUP in the logical plan. The MapReduce task corresponding to the GROUP operator has a Combiner as well. It must be noted that the GROUP operation happens in the Map task.

Pig modes

The user can run Pig in two modes:

- **Local Mode**: With access to a single machine, all files are installed and run using a localhost and filesystem.
- **MapReduce Mode**: This is the default mode, which requires access to a Hadoop cluster.

In Pig, there are three modes of execution:

- **Interactive mode or grunt mode**
- **Batch mode or script mode**
- **Embedded mode**: Embed Pig commands in a host language such as Python or JavaScript and run the program

These modes of execution can be either executed in the Local mode or in the MapReduce mode.

Grunt shell

Grunt is Pig's interactive shell. It can be used to enter Pig Latin interactively and provides a shell for users to interact with HDFS.

For Local mode:

Specify local mode using the -x flag:

```
$ pig -x local
```

For MapReduce mode:

Point Pig to a remote cluster by placing HADOOP_CONF_DIR on PIG_CLASSPATH.

> HADOOP_CONF_DIR is the directory containing the hadoop-site.xml, hdfs-site.xml, and mapred-site.xml files
>
> Example: $ export PIG_CLASSPATH=<path_to_hadoop_conf_dir>

This is given here:

```
$ pig
grunt>
```

Input data

We will be using the movies_data.csv file as a dataset for exploring Pig. The input file has the following fields and sample data:

ID	Name	Year	Rating	Duration in sec
40146	Oscar's Oasis: Chicken Charmer Top Gun Lizard: Wanted Power of Love	2011		1601
40147	Transformers: Rescue Bots: Season 1: Return of the Dino Bot	2011		1324
40148	Plankton Invasion: Operation Winkle Zone Operation Cod-Tagion Operation Hardshell	2012		1262

ID	Name	Year	Rating	Duration in sec
40149	Transformers: Rescue Bots: Season 1: Deep Trouble	2011		1324
40150	Trailer: Lift the Veil	2012	3.6	69
40151	Trailer: Pain	2012	3.6	52
40152	Todd and the Book of Pure Evil	2010	3.9	
40153	Trailer: House of Cards	2012	3.7	148

Loading data

For loading your data in Pig, we use the LOAD command and map it to an alias of relation (as movies in this example), which can read data from the filesystem or HDFS and load it for processing within Pig. Different storage handlers are available in Pig for handling different types of records by mentioning USING and the storage handler function; few of the frequently used storage handler functions are:

- PigStorage which is used for structured text files with a delimiter that can be specified and is the default storage handler
- HBaseStorage which is used for handling data from HBase tables
- BinStorage which is used for binary and machine readable formats
- JSONStorage which is used for handling JSON data and a schema that should be specified
- TextLoader which is used for unstructured data in UTF-8

If we do not mention any handler by default, PigStorage will be used by default, and PigStorage and TextStorage will support the compression files gzip and bzip.

Example:

```
grunt> movies = LOAD '/user/biadmin/shiva/movies_data.csv' USING
  PigStorage(',') as (id,name,year,rating,duration);
```

We can use schemas to assign types to fields:

```
A = LOAD 'data' AS (name, age, gpa);
  // name, age, gpa default to bytearrays
A = LOAD 'data' AS (name:chararray, age:int, gpa:float);
  // name is now a String (chararray), age is integer and gpa is
    float
```

Dump

The dump command is very useful to interactively view the values stored in the relation and writes the output to the console. DUMP doesn't save the data:

Example:

```
grunt> DUMP movies;
INFO  [JobControl] org.apache.hadoop.mapreduce.lib.input.FileInputFormat
- Total input paths to process : 1
INFO  [main] org.apache.hadoop.mapreduce.lib.input.FileInputFormat    -
Total input paths to process : 1
(1,The Nightmare Before Christmas,1993,3.9,4568)
(2,The Mummy,1932,3.5,4388)
(3,Orphans of the Storm,1921,3.2,9062)
(4,The Object of Beauty,1991,2.8,6150)
(5,Night Tide,1963,2.8,5126)
(6,One Magic Christmas,1985,3.8,5333)
(7,Muriel's Wedding,1994,3.5,6323)
```

Store

The store command is used to write or continue with the data. Pig starts a job only when a DUMP or STORE is encountered. We can use the handlers mentioned in LOAD with STORE too.

Example:

```
grunt> STORE movies INTO '/temp' USING PigStorage(','); //This will
  write contents of movies to HDFS in /temp location
```

FOREACH generate

A FOREACH operation is used to apply a column-level expression in each record of the relation. It is quite powerful to even allow some columns from the relation, and we can use UDF as an expression in FOREACH.

Example:

```
grunt> movie_duration = FOREACH movies GENERATE name,
  (double)(duration/60);
```

Filter

Filter is used to get rows matching the expression criteria.

Example:

```
grunt> movies_greater_than_four = FILTER movies BY (float)rating>4.0;
grunt> DUMP movies_greater_than_four;
```

We can use multiple conditions with filters and Boolean operators (AND, OR, NOT):

```
grunt> movies_greater_than_four_and_2012 = FILTER movies BY (float)
rating>4.0 AND year > 2012;
grunt> DUMP movies_greater_than_four_and_2012;
INFO   [JobControl] org.apache.hadoop.mapreduce.lib.input.FileInputFormat
- Total input paths to process : 1
WARN   [main] org.apache.pig.data.SchemaTupleBackend        -
SchemaTupleBackend has already been initialized
INFO   [main] org.apache.hadoop.mapreduce.lib.input.FileInputFormat        -
Total input paths to process : 1
(22148,House of Cards: Season 1,2013,4.4,)
(22403,House of Cards,2013,4.4,)
(37138,Orange Is the New Black: Season 1,2013,4.5,)
(37141,Orange Is the New Black,2013,4.5,)
(37174,The Following: Season 1,2013,4.1,)
(37239,The Following,2013,4.1,)
(37318,The Carrie Diaries,2013,4.3,)
(37320,The Carrie Diaries: Season 1,2013,4.3,)
(37589,Safe Haven,2013,4.2,6936)
```

Group By

The Group By command is used to create groups of records with a key. Group By relations are used to work with the aggregation functions on the grouped data.

The syntax for Group By is as follows:

```
alias = GROUP alias { ALL | BY expression} [, alias ALL | BY
expression ...] [PARALLEL n];
```

For example:

- To `Group` `By` (employee start year at Salesforce)

  ```
  grunt> grouped_by_year = group movies by year;
  ```

- Or `Group` `By` multiple fields:

  ```
  B = GROUP A BY (age, employeesince);
  ```

Limit

The `Limit` command limits the number of output tuples in a relation, but the tuples return can change in a different execution of the command. For a specific tuple, we have to use `ORDER` along with `LIMIT`, which will return the ordered set of tuples.

Example:

```
grunt> movies_limit_10 = LIMIT movies 10;

grunt> DUMP movies_limit_10;

INFO  [JobControl] org.apache.hadoop.mapreduce.lib.input.FileInputFormat
- Total input paths to process : 1

INFO  [JobControl] org.apache.hadoop.mapreduce.lib.input.FileInputFormat
- Total input paths to process : 1

WARN  [main] org.apache.pig.data.SchemaTupleBackend       -
SchemaTupleBackend has already been initialized

INFO  [main] org.apache.hadoop.mapreduce.lib.input.FileInputFormat      -
Total input paths to process : 1

(1,The Nightmare Before Christmas,1993,3.9,4568)

(2,The Mummy,1932,3.5,4388)

(3,Orphans of the Storm,1921,3.2,9062)

(4,The Object of Beauty,1991,2.8,6150)

(5,Night Tide,1963,2.8,5126)

(6,One Magic Christmas,1985,3.8,5333)

(7,Muriel's Wedding,1994,3.5,6323)

(8,Mother's Boys,1994,3.4,5733)

(9,Nosferatu: Original Version,1929,3.5,5651)

(10,Nick of Time,1995,3.4,5333)
```

Aggregation

Pig provides a bunch of aggregation functions such as:

- AVG
- COUNT
- COUNT_STAR
- SUM
- MAX
- MIN

Example:

```
grunt> count_by_year = FOREACH grouped_by_year GENERATE group,
COUNT(movies);

grunt> DUMP count_by_year;
INFO   [JobControl] org.apache.hadoop.mapreduce.lib.input.FileInputFormat
- Total input paths to process : 1

INFO   [main] org.apache.hadoop.mapreduce.lib.input.FileInputFormat       -
Total input paths to process : 1

(1913,3)
(1914,20)
.

.

 (2009,4451)
(2010,5107)
(2011,5511)
(2012,4339)
(2013,981)
(2014,1)
```

Cogroup

Cogroup is a generalization of group. Instead of collecting records of one input based on a key, it collects records of *n* inputs based on a key. The result is a record with a key and a bag for each input. Each bag contains all records from that input that have the given value for the key:

```
$ cat > owners.csv
adam,cat
```

```
adam,dog
alex,fish
alice,cat
steve,dog

$ cat > pets.csv
nemo,fish
fido,dog
rex,dog
paws,cat
wiskers,cat

grunt> owners = LOAD 'owners.csv'
>>      USING PigStorage(',')
>>      AS (owner:chararray,animal:chararray);

grunt> pets = LOAD 'pets.csv'
>>      USING PigStorage(',')
>>      AS (name:chararray,animal:chararray);

grunt> grouped = COGROUP owners BY animal, pets by animal;
grunt> DUMP grouped;
```

This will group each table based on the animal column. For each animal, it will create a bag of matching rows from both tables. For this example, we get the results, as shown in the following table:

group	owners	pets
cat	{(adam,cat),(alice,cat)}	{(paws,cat),(wiskers,cat)}
dog	{(adam,dog),(steve,dog)}	{(fido,dog),(rex,dog)}
fish	{(alex,fish)}	{(nemo,fish)}

DESCRIBE

The DESCRIBE command gives the schema of a relation, as shown here:

```
grunt> Describe grouped;
grouped: {group: chararray,owners: {(owner: chararray,animal:
  chararray)},pets: {(name: chararray,animal: chararray)}}
```

EXPLAIN

The EXPLAIN command on a relation shows how the Pig script is going to get executed. It shows the Logical plan, the Physical plan, and the MapReduce plan of the relation. We can use the EXPLAIN command to study the optimizations that have gone into the plans. This command can be used to optimize the script further:

```
grunt> explain grouped;
#-----------------------------------------------
# New Logical Plan:
#-----------------------------------------------
grouped: (Name: LOStore Schema: group#107:chararray,owners#108:bag{#118:t
uple(owner#94:chararray,animal#95:chararray)},pets#110:bag{#119:tuple(nam
e#96:chararray,animal#97:chararray)})
|
|---grouped: (Name: LOCogroup Schema: group#107:chararray,owners#108:bag{
#118:tuple(owner#94:chararray,animal#95:chararray)},pets#110:bag{#119:tup
le(name#96:chararray,animal#97:chararray)})
    |   |
    |   animal:(Name: Project Type: chararray Uid: 95 Input: 0 Column: 1)
    |   |
    |   animal:(Name: Project Type: chararray Uid: 97 Input: 1 Column: 1)
    |
    |---owners: (Name: LOForEach Schema: owner#94:chararray,animal#95:cha
rarray)
        |   |   |
        |   |   (Name: LOGenerate[false,false] Schema: owner#94:
chararray,animal#95:chararray)ColumnPrune:InputUids=[95, 94]
ColumnPrune:OutputUids=[95, 94]
        |   |   |   |
        |   |   |   (Name: Cast Type: chararray Uid: 94)
        |   |   |   |
        |   |   |   |---owner:(Name: Project Type: bytearray Uid: 94 Input: 0
Column: (*))
```

```
|    |    |    |
|    |    |         (Name: Cast Type: chararray Uid: 95)
|    |    |    |
|    |    |    |---animal:(Name: Project Type: bytearray Uid: 95 Input:
1 Column: (*))
|    |    |
|    |    |---(Name: LOInnerLoad[0] Schema: owner#94:bytearray)
|    |    |
|    |    |---(Name: LOInnerLoad[1] Schema: animal#95:bytearray)
|    |
|    |---owners: (Name: LOLoad Schema: owner#94:bytearray,animal#95:by
tearray)RequiredFields:null
|
|---pets: (Name: LOForEach Schema: name#96:chararray,animal#97:charar
ray)
          |    |
          |         (Name: LOGenerate[false,false] Schema: name#96:chararray,anim
al#97:chararray)ColumnPrune:InputUids=[96, 97]ColumnPrune:OutputUids=[96,
97]
          |    |    |
          |    |         (Name: Cast Type: chararray Uid: 96)
          |    |    |
          |    |    |---name:(Name: Project Type: bytearray Uid: 96 Input: 0
Column: (*))
          |    |    |
          |    |         (Name: Cast Type: chararray Uid: 97)
          |    |    |
          |    |    |---animal:(Name: Project Type: bytearray Uid: 97 Input:
1 Column: (*))
          |    |
          |    |---(Name: LOInnerLoad[0] Schema: name#96:bytearray)
          |    |
          |    |---(Name: LOInnerLoad[1] Schema: animal#97:bytearray)
          |
          |---pets: (Name: LOLoad Schema: name#96:bytearray,animal#97:bytea
rray)RequiredFields:null


#-----------------------------------------------
```

```
# Physical Plan:
#-----------------------------------------------
grouped: Store(fakefile:org.apache.pig.builtin.PigStorage) - scope-76
|
|---grouped: Package[tuple]{chararray} - scope-71
    |
    |---grouped: Global Rearrange[tuple] - scope-70
        |
        |---grouped: Local Rearrange[tuple]{chararray}(false) - scope-72
        |   |   |
        |   |   Project[chararray][1] - scope-73
        |   |
        |   |---owners: New For Each(false,false)[bag] - scope-61
        |           |   |
        |           |   Cast[chararray] - scope-56
        |           |   |
        |           |   |---Project[bytearray][0] - scope-55
        |           |   |
        |           |   Cast[chararray] - scope-59
        |           |   |
        |           |   |---Project[bytearray][1] - scope-58
        |           |
        |           |---owners: Load(file:///home/opt/pig/bin/owners.
csv:PigStorage(',')) - scope-54
        |
        |---grouped: Local Rearrange[tuple]{chararray}(false) - scope-74
            |   |
            |   Project[chararray][1] - scope-75
            |
            |---pets: New For Each(false,false)[bag] - scope-69
                |   |
                |   Cast[chararray] - scope-64
                |   |
                |   |---Project[bytearray][0] - scope-63
                |   |
                |   Cast[chararray] - scope-67
```

```
    |     |
    |     |---Project[bytearray] [1] - scope-66
    |
    |---pets: Load(file:///home/opt/pig/bin/pets.
csv:PigStorage(',')) - scope-62


#--------------------------------------------------
# Map Reduce Plan
#--------------------------------------------------
MapReduce node scope-79
Map Plan
Union[tuple] - scope-80
|
|---grouped: Local Rearrange[tuple]{chararray}(false) - scope-72
|   |   |
|   |     Project[chararray] [1] - scope-73
|   |
|   |---owners: New For Each(false,false)[bag] - scope-61
|   |     |   |
|   |     |   Cast[chararray] - scope-56
|   |     |   |
|   |     |   |---Project[bytearray] [0] - scope-55
|   |     |   |
|   |     |   Cast[chararray] - scope-59
|   |     |   |
|   |     |   |---Project[bytearray] [1] - scope-58
|   |     |
|   |     |---owners: Load(file:///home/opt/pig/bin/owners.
csv:PigStorage(',')) - scope-54
|
|---grouped: Local Rearrange[tuple]{chararray}(false) - scope-74
    |   |
    |     Project[chararray] [1] - scope-75
    |
    |---pets: New For Each(false,false)[bag] - scope-69
        |   |
```

```
    |     Cast[chararray] - scope-64
    |     |
    |     |---Project[bytearray][0] - scope-63
    |     |
    |     Cast[chararray] - scope-67
    |     |
    |     |---Project[bytearray][1] - scope-66
    |
    |---pets: Load(file:///home/opt/pig/bin/pets.csv:PigStorage(','))
- scope-62--------
Reduce Plan
grouped: Store(fakefile:org.apache.pig.builtin.PigStorage) - scope-76
|
|---grouped: Package[tuple]{chararray} - scope-71--------
Global sort: false
----------------
```

ILLUSTRATE

The ILLUSTRATE command is perhaps the most important development aid. ILLUSTRATE on a relation samples the data and applies the query on it. This can save a lot of time during the debugging process. The sample is significantly smaller than the data making the code, test, and, debug cycle very fast. In many situations, JOIN or FILTER operators may not yield any output on a sample of the data. In such cases, ILLUSTRATE manufactures records that pass through these operators and inserts them into the sample dataset:

```
grunt> illustrate grouped;
```

owners	owner:chararray	animal:chararray
	steve	dog
	adam	dog

pets	name:chararray	animal:chararray
	fido	dog
	rex	dog

```
--------------------------------------------------------
----------------------------------------------------------
----------------------------------------------------------
-----------------------------
| grouped       | group:chararray     | owners:bag{:tuple(owner:chararray,a
nimal:chararray)}                       | pets:bag{:tuple(name:chararray,animal
:chararray)}                           |
----------------------------------------------------------
----------------------------------------------------------
-----------------------------
|               | dog                 | {(steve, dog), (adam, dog)}
| {(fido, dog), (rex, dog)}                                              |
----------------------------------------------------------
----------------------------------------------------------
-----------------------------
```

Pig is widely used in data flows and ETL, hence scripting like Pig Latin languages helps to design the flow easily.

Hive

Hive provides a data warehouse environment in Hadoop with a SQL-like wrapper and also translates the SQL commands in MapReduce jobs for processing. SQL commands in Hive are called as HiveQL, which doesn't support the SQL 92 dialect and should not be assumed to support all the keywords, as the whole idea is to hide the complexity of MapReduce programming and perform analysis on the data.

Hive can also act as an analytical interface with other systems as most of the systems integrate well with Hive. Hive cannot be used for handling transactions, as it doesn't provide row-level updates and real-time queries.

The Hive architecture

Hive architecture has different components such as:

- **Driver**: Driver manages the lifecycle of a HiveQL statement as it moves through Hive and also maintains a session handle for session statistics.
- **Metastore**: Metastore stores the system catalog and metadata about tables, columns, partitions, and so on.
- **Query Compiler**: It compiles HiveQL into a DAG of optimized map/reduce tasks.

- **Execution Engine**: It executes the tasks produced by the compiler in a proper dependency order. The execution engine interacts with the underlying Hadoop instance.

- **HiveServer2**: It provides a thrift interface and a JDBC/ODBC server and provides a way of integrating Hive with other applications and supports multi-client concurrency and authentication.

- Client components such as the Command Line Interface (CLI), the web UI, and drivers. The drivers are the JDBC/ODBC drivers provided by vendors and other appropriate drivers.

The process flow of HiveQL is described here:

- A HiveQL statement can be submitted from the CLI, the web UI, or an external client using interfaces such as thrift, ODBC, or JDBC.

- The driver first passes the query to the compiler where it goes through the typical parse, type check, and semantic analysis phases, using the metadata stored in the Metastore.

- The compiler generates a logical plan which is then optimized through a simple rule-based optimizer. Finally, an optimized plan in the form of a DAG of MapReduce tasks and HDFS tasks is generated. The execution engine then executes these tasks in the order of their dependencies by using Hadoop.

Let us check more details on the Metastore, the Query Compiler, and the Execution Engine.

Metastore

The Metastore stores all the details about the tables, partitions, schemas, columns, types, and so on. It acts as a system catalog for Hive. It can be called from clients from different programming languages, as the details can be queried using Thrift. Metastore is very critical for Hive without which the structure design details cannot be retrieved and data cannot be accessed. Hence, Metastore is backed up regularly.

Metastore can become a bottleneck in Hive, so an isolated JVM process is advised with a local JDBC database like MySQL. Hive ensures that Metastore is not directly accessed by Mappers and Reducers of a job; instead it is passed through an xml plan that is generated by the compiler and contains information that is needed at runtime.

The Query compiler

The query compiler uses the metadata stored by Metastore to process the HiveQL statements to generate an execution plan. The query compiler performs the following steps:

- **Parse**: The query compiler parses the statement.

- **Type checking and semantic analysis**: In this phase, the compiler uses the metadata to check the type compatibility in expressions and semantics of the statement. After the checks are validated and no errors are found, the compiler builds a logical plan for the statement.

- **Optimization**: The compiler optimizes the logical plan and creates a DAG to pass the result of one chain to the next and tries to optimize the plan by applying different rules, if possible, for logical steps.

The Execution engine

The execution engine executes the optimized plan. It executes the plan step by step, considering the dependent task to complete for every task in the plan. The results of tasks are stored in a temporary location and in the final step the data is moved to the desired location.

Data types and schemas

Hive supports all the primitive numeric data types such as TINYINT, SMALLINT, INT, BIGINT, FLOAT, DOUBLE, and DECIMAL. In addition to these primitive data types, Hive also supports string types such as CHAR, VARCHAR, and STRING data types. Like SQL, time indicator data types such as TIMESTAMP and DATE are present. The BOOLEAN and BINARY miscellaneous types are available too.

A number of complex data types are also available. The complex types can be composed from other primitive or complex types. The complex types available are:

- **STRUCT**: These are groupings of data elements similar to a C-struct. The dot notation is used to dereference elements within a struct. A field within column C defined as a STRUCT {x INT, y STRING} can be accessed as A.x or A.y.

  Syntax: STRUCT<field_name : data_type>

- **MAP**: These are key value data types. Providing the key within square braces can help access a value. A value of a map column M that maps from key x to value y can be accessed by M[x].There is no restriction on the type stored by the value, though the key needs to be of a primitive type.

  Syntax: `MAP<primitive_type, data_type>`

- **ARRAY**: These are lists that can be randomly accessed through their position. The syntax to access an array element is the same as a map. But what goes into the square braces is a zero-based index of the element.

  Syntax: `ARRAY<data_type>`

- **UNION**: There is a union type available in Hive. It can hold an element of one of the data types specified in the union.

  Syntax: `UNIONTYPE<data_type1, data_type2…>`

Installing Hive

Hive can be installed by downloading and unpacking a tarball, or you can download the source code and build Hive using Maven (release 0.13 and later) or Ant (release 0.12 and earlier).

The Hive installation process has these requirements:

- Java 1.7 (preferred) or Java 1.6
- Hadoop 2.*x* (preferred) or 1.*x*. Hive versions up to 0.13 but it also supports 0.20.*x* or 0.23.*x*
- Hive is commonly used in production in Linux and Windows environments

Start by downloading the most recent stable release of Hive from one of the Apache download mirrors (see Hive Releases).

Next, you need to unpack the tarball. This will result in the creation of a subdirectory named hive-x.y.z (where x.y.z is the release number):

```
$ tar -xzvf hive-x.y.z.tar.gz
```

Set the environment variable `HIVE_HOME` to point to the installation directory:

```
$ cd hive-x.y.z
$ export HIVE_HOME={{pwd}}
```

Finally, add `$HIVE_HOME/bin` to your `Path`:

```
$ export PATH=$HIVE_HOME/bin:$PATH
```

Starting Hive shell

For using Hive shell, we should follow these steps:

1. The user must create `/tmp` and `/user/hive/warehouse` and set them as `chmod g+w` in HDFS before a table can be created in Hive. The commands to perform this setup are these:

```
$HADOOP_HOME/bin$ ./hadoop dfs -mkdir /tmp

$HADOOP_HOME/bin$ ./hadoop dfs -mkdir /user/hive/warehouse

$HADOOP_HOME/bin$ ./hadoop dfs -chmod g+w /tmp

$HADOOP_HOME/bin$ ./hadoop dfs -chmod g+w
  /user/hive/warehouse
```

2. To use the Hive command-line interface (`cli`) from the shell, use the following script:

```
$HIVE_HOME/bin$ ./hive
```

HiveQL

HiveQL has a wide range of Hive built-in operators, Hive built-in functions, Hive built-in aggregate functions, UDF, and UDAF for user-defined functions.

DDL (Data Definition Language) operations

Let's start with the DDL operation commands which are:

- `Create database`: The `Create database` command is used for creating a database in Hive. Example:

```
hive> Create database shiva;

OK

Time taken: 0.764 seconds
```

- `Show database`: The `Show database` command is used to list down all the existing databases in Hive. Example:

```
hive> show databases;


OK

default

shiva

Time taken: 4.458 seconds, Fetched: 2 row(s)
```

- Use database: The Use database command is used to select a database for the session. Example:

```
hive> use shiva;
```

- Create table: The Create table is used to create a Hive table. In the create table command, we can specify whether a table is Managed or External, if it requires partitioning, bucketing, and other important features in the Hive table. An example of a simple "create table" option is this:

```
hive> Create table person (name STRING , add STRING);
```

The Create table command has many options which we will see in the create table section given next. The preceding command is the simplest form of table creation in Hive.

The Create command has a lot of options for specific cases and its requirements are:

```
CREATE [EXTERNAL] TABLE [IF NOT EXISTS] table_name
[(col_name data_type [COMMENT col_comment], ...)]
[COMMENT table_comment]
[PARTITIONED BY (col_name data_type [COMMENT col_comment], ...)]
[CLUSTERED BY (col_name, col_name, ...) [SORTED BY (col_name [ASC|DESC],
...)] INTO num_buckets BUCKETS]
[ROW FORMAT row_format] [STORED AS file_format]
[LOCATION hdfs_path]
[TBLPROPERTIES (property_name=property_value, ...)]
[AS select_statement]
```

- **Create table**: This command creates a table with the given table name and the following options explained:
    - **IF NOT EXISTS**: This command is used to skip the error if a table or view with the same name already exists.
    - **The EXTERNAL keyword**: As we discussed earlier, this command allows us to create a table and we have to provide a LOCATION for this.
    - **ROW FORMAT**: We can use custom SerDe or native SerDe while creating a table. A native SerDe is used if ROW FORMAT is not specified or ROW FORMAT DELIMITED is specified. You can use the DELIMITED clause to read delimited files.

- ° **STORED AS**: We can use TEXTFILE if the data needs to be stored as plain text files. Use STORED AS SEQUENCEFILE if the data needs to be compressed.

- ° **PARTITIONED BY**: Partitioned tables can be created using the PARTITIONED BY clause.

- ° **CLUSTERED BY**: Further, tables or partitions can be bucketed using columns, and data can be sorted within that bucket via SORT BY columns. This can improve the performance of certain kinds of queries.

- ° **TBLPROPERTIES**: This clause allows you to tag the table definition with your own metadata key/value pairs.

- **Show tables**: The Show tables command is used to list all the tables present in the database:

```
hive>Show tables;

OK

person

Time taken: 0.057 seconds, Fetched: 1 row(s)


hive>Show tables '.*n';-- List all the table end that end with s.


OK

person

Time taken: 0.057 seconds, Fetched: 1 row(s)
```

- **Describe table**: The describe table command is used to get useful information about the table and the columns.

```
hive> describe person;

OK

name                      string              None
add                       string              None
Time taken: 0.181 seconds, Fetched: 2 row(s)
```

- **Alter table**: The Alter table command is used to change table metadata and to add partitioning or bucketing.

```
hive> Alter table person ADD COLUMNS (PNO  INT);

OK

Time taken: 0.334 seconds
```

- **Drop table**: The `drop table` command is used to remove the table from Hive metadata; if the table is Hive-managed, then this command will also remove the data, and if it's external then only the Hive metadata is removed.

```
hive>drop table person;
```

DML (Data Manipulation Language) operations

Now, let's look at the DML operation commands:

Load data: A file in Hive can be loaded from local, as well as from HDFS; by default Hive will look in HDFS.

The input data we are using is simple personal data having `Name`, `add`, and `pno`; a sample of this data is like this:

Name	add	pno
Alvin Joyner	678-8957 Nisi Avenue	1
Jasper G. Robertson	8336 Tincidunt Av.	2
Deirdre Fulton	624-9370 Nisl. Street	3
Hillary Craig	Ap #198-3439 Id Av.	4
Blaze Carr	Ap #283-9985 Purus Road	5

Look at the following command:

```
hive>LOAD DATA INPATH 'hdfs://localhost:9000/user/hive/shiva/PersonData.csv' OVERWRITE INTO TABLE person;


Loading data to table shiva.person
OK
Time taken: 0.721 seconds
```

The preceding command will load data from an HDFS file/directory to the table, and the process of loading data from HDFS will result in moving the file/directory.

For Local Data load, use the following code:

```
hive>LOAD DATA LOCAL INPATH './examples/shiva/file1.txt' OVERWRITE
    INTO TABLE person;
```

We can also load the data with PARTITION:

```
hive>LOAD DATA LOCAL INPATH './examples/ shiva /file2.txt'

    OVERWRITE INTO TABLE person PARTITION (date='26-02-2014');
```

The SQL operation

Querying the data in Hive can be done as shown in the following sections:

SELECT: SELECT is the projection operator in SQL. The clauses used for this function are:

- SELECT scans the table specified by the FROM clause
- WHERE gives the condition of what to filter
- GROUP BY gives a list of columns which then specify how to aggregate the records
- CLUSTER BY, DISTRIBUTE BY, and SORT BY specify the sort order and algorithm
- LIMIT specifies the # of records to retrieve:

  ```
  SELECT [ALL | DISTINCT] select_expr, select_expr,

  FROM table_reference

  [WHERE where_condition]

  [GROUP BY col_list]

  [HAVING having_condition]

  [CLUSTER BY col_list | [DISTRIBUTE BY col_list] [SORT BY
    col_list]]

  [LIMIT number];
  ```

Example:

```
hive>select * from person where name = 'Alvin Joyner';


Total MapReduce jobs = 1

Launching Job 1 out of 1

Number of reduce tasks is set to 0 since there's no reduce operator

Starting Job = job_201503051113_2664, Tracking URL = http://machine76.
bigdatadomain.com:50030/jobdetails.jsp?jobid=job_201503051113_2664

Hadoop job information for Stage-1: number of mappers: 1; number of
reducers: 0

2015-03-24 14:52:54,541 Stage-1 map = 0%,  reduce = 0%

2015-03-24 14:52:58,570 Stage-1 map = 100%,  reduce = 0%, Cumulative CPU
2.57 sec

2015-03-24 14:52:59,579 Stage-1 map = 100%,  reduce = 100%, Cumulative
CPU 2.57 sec

MapReduce Total cumulative CPU time: 2 seconds 570 msec
```

```
Ended Job = job_201503051113_2664
```

```
MapReduce Jobs Launched:
```

```
Job 0: Map: 1    Cumulative CPU: 2.57 sec    HDFS Read: 4502 HDFS Write: 0
SUCCESS
```

```
Total MapReduce CPU Time Spent: 2 seconds 570 msec
```

```
OK
```

```
Time taken: 12.53 seconds
```

Joins

HiveQL supports the following types of joins:

- JOIN
- LEFT OUTER JOIN
- RIGHT OUTER JOIN
- FULL OUTER JOIN

Only `equi join` is supported in HiveQL; non-equality condition joins cannot be executed. The default join option in HiveQL is equi join, whereas in SQL the default is inner join; one syntactic difference in also present which is we have to mention LEFT `OUTER JOIN` and `RIGHT OUTER JOIN` whereas in `SQL LEFT JOIN` and `RIGHT JOIN` works.

HiveQL is converted into MapReduce jobs, hence we have to design the query keeping the MapReduce paradigm in mind. The joins are executed as Mapside join or reduce side join depending on the parser and the optimization plan, hence the thumb rule is to join the smaller tables earlier to avoid the huge amount of data transfer or process and join the larger table at the last. The reason behind this, is that in every MapReduce stage of the joint, the last table is streamlined through the reducers; whereas the others are buffered.

Example:

```
Hive> SELECT a.val1, a.val2, b.val, c.val
   > FROM a
   > JOIN b ON (a.key = b.key)
   > LEFT OUTER JOIN c ON (a.key = c.key);
```

As mentioned in the Hive wiki, the following conditions are not supported:

- Union followed by a MapJoin
- Lateral View followed by a MapJoin

- Reduce Sink (Group By/Join/Sort By/Cluster By/Distribute By) followed by MapJoin
- MapJoin followed by Union
- MapJoin followed by Join
- MapJoin followed by MapJoin

Aggregations

HiveQL supports aggregations and also allows for multiple aggregations to be done at the same time. The possible aggregators are:

- `count(*)`, `count(expr)`, `count(DISTINCT expr[, expr_.])`
- `sum(col)`, `sum(DISTINCT col)`
- `avg(col)`, `avg(DISTINCT col)`
- `min(col)`
- `max(col)`

Example:

```
hive> SELECT a, sum(b) FROM t1
    > GROUP BY a;
```

Hive also supports map-side aggregation for `Group By` for improving the performance but would require more memory. If we set `hive.map.aggr` as true (the default is false), then Hive will do the first-level aggregation directly in the map task.

```
hive> set hive.map.aggr=true;
hive> SELECT COUNT(*) FROM table2;
```

Built-in functions

Hive has numerous built-in functions and some of its widely used functions are:

- `concat(string A, string B,...)`
- `substr(string A, int start)`
- `round(double a)`
- `upper(string A), lower(string A)`
- `trim(string A)`
- `to_date(string timestamp)`
- `year(string date), month(string date), day(string date)`

Custom UDF (User Defined Functions)

We can create our own Custom UDF functions and use it in Hive queries. Hive provides an interface for user-defined functions where custom functions can be written in Java and deployed, which can be used as a function in HiveQL. The steps to be performed for Custom UDF are these:

1. Create a new Java class that extends UDF with one or more methods named evaluate:

```
import org.apache.hadoop.hive.ql.exec.UDF;
import org.apache.hadoop.io.Text;
public class LowerUDF extends UDF
{
  public Text evaluate(final Text s)
  {
    if (s == null) { return null; }
    return new Text(s.toString().toLowerCase());
  }
}
```

2. Now, compile the function and make jar.

3. Deploy jars for user-defined functions:

```
hive> add jar my_jar.jar;
```

Added `my_jar.jar` to class path

4. Once Hive has started with your jars in the classpath, the final step is to register your function:

```
create temporary function my_lowerUDF as 'Lower';
```

5. Now, you can start using it.

```
hive> select my_lowerUDF(title), sum(freq) from titles group
  by my_lowerUDF(title);
```

Managing tables – external versus managed

Hive has the flexibility to manage only metadata or metadata along with the data. In Hive the two types of data management are:

- **Managed**: Metadata along with data will be managed by Hive.
- **External**: Only metadata will be stored and managed by Hive.

The managed table in Hive should be used if we want Hive to manage the lifecycle of the table, and data should be used in the case of a temporary table.

The advantages of using an external table are:

- We can use a custom location like HBase, Cassandra, and so on.

- Data can be processed by the other system which can avoid locking, while processing and improving the performance

- In the DROP table command, only the metadata will be deleted and the data will not be deleted.

SerDe

One of the important benefits of using Hadoop is its flexibility to store and provide interfaces to process semi-structured and unstructured data. Hive can also be used for processing this data; Hive does it due to its complex data types and SerDe properties. SerDe is a Serializer and Deserializer interface which can allow marshalling and unmarshalling of string or binary data in Java objects, which can be used by Hive for reading and writing in tables. Hive has some built-in SerDe libraries such as Avro, ORC, RegEx, Thrift, Parquet, and CSV; it also has a third party SerDe like that of JSON SerDe provided by Amazon.

We can also write our custom SerDe. For writing a custom SerDe class, we have to override some methods:

- `public void initialize (Configuration conf, Properties tbl) throws SerDeException`: The `initialize()` method is called only once and we can get and set some commonly used information from the table properties such as column types and names.

- `public Writable serialize (Object obj, ObjectInspector oi) throws SerDeException`: The `serialize()` method should have the logic of seralization that takes a Java object representing a row of data and generates a writable interface object which can be serialized.

- `public Class<? extends Writable> getSerializedClass ():` The `getSerializedClass()` returns the return type class of the serialized object.

- `public Object deserialize (Writable blob) throws SerDeException`: The `deserialize()` should have the deserialization logic.

- `public ObjectInspector getObjectInspector () throws SerDeException`: The `ObjectInspectors` are Hive objects that are used to describe and examine complex type hierarchies.

- `public SerDeStats getSerDeStats ()`: They override to support some statistics.

Let's look at a code for implementing Custom SerDe:

```
public class CustomSerDe implements SerDe {

  private StructTypeInfo rowTypeInfo;
  private ObjectInspector rowOI;
  private List<String> colNames;
  Object[] outputFields;
  Text outputRowText;
  private List<Object> row = new ArrayList<Object>();

  @Override
  public void initialize(Configuration conf, Properties tbl)
    throws SerDeException {
    // Get a list of the table's column names.
    String colNamesStr = tbl.getProperty(Constants.LIST_COLUMNS);
    colNames = Arrays.asList(colNamesStr.split(","));

    // Get a list of TypeInfos for the columns. This list lines up
      with
    // the list of column names.
    String colTypesStr =
      tbl.getProperty(Constants.LIST_COLUMN_TYPES);
    List<TypeInfo> colTypes =
      TypeInfoUtils.getTypeInfosFromTypeString(colTypesStr);
    rowTypeInfo =
      (StructTypeInfo) TypeInfoFactory.getStructTypeInfo(colNames,
        colTypes);
    rowOI =
      TypeInfoUtils.getStandardJavaObjectInspectorFromTypeInfo
        (rowTypeInfo);
  }

  @Override
  public Object deserialize(Writable blob) throws SerDeException {
    row.clear();
    // Implement the logic of Deserialization
    return row;
  }

  @Override
  public ObjectInspector getObjectInspector() throws SerDeException {
    return rowOI;
  }

  @Override
  public SerDeStats getSerDeStats() {
```

```
      return null;
    }

    @Override
    public Class<? extends Writable> getSerializedClass() {
      return Text.class;
    }

    @Override
    public Writable serialize(Object obj, ObjectInspector oi)
        throws SerDeException {
      // Implement Logic of Serialization
      return outputRowText;
    }
  }
}
```

We have to create a jar file of the class and put it in the Hive server. We can then use the SerDe while creating the table, as shown in the following code:

```
CREATE EXTERNAL TABLE IF NOT EXISTS my_table (
  field1 string, field2 int, field3 string, field4 double)
ROW FORMAT SERDE 'org.apache.hadoop.hive.contrib.serde2.
  CustomSerDe' LOCATION '/path-to/my_table/';
```

Partitioning

Hive supports partitioning of data, which can be used for distributing data horizontally. For example, if we have a large transaction table which frequently queries with respect to a year or range of months, then we can partition the table with PARTITIONED BY (year INT, month INT) while creating one.

Hive manages the data by creating subdirectories as the structure of partition fields such as:

/DB/Table/Year/Month/.

/db/table/2014/11/.

/db/table/2014/12/.

/db/table/2015/1/.

/db/table/2015/2/.

Partitioning works on managed and external tables and is advised for very large tables which can limit the files to be processed and provide a huge advantage to improve the performance.

Partitioning should be done carefully as, it can have the following downsides:

- If partition columns are not selected properly, then it can unevenly divide the data and query execution will not be optimized.

- If the partition hierarchy levels become high, then the recursively scanning the directories will be more expensive than full data scan.

Bucketing

We just discussed the fact about partitioning that it can unevenly distribute the data, but usually it is very less likely to get even distribution. But, we can achieve almost even distributed data for processing using bucketing. Bucketing has a value of data into a bucket due to which the same value records can be present in the same bucket, and a bucket can have multiple groups of values. Bucketing provides control to a number of files, as we have to mention the number of buckets while using bucketing in `create table` using `CLUSTERED BY (month) INTO #noofBuckets BUCKETS`.

For even distribution of data, we should set `hive.enforce.bucketing = true`. Bucketing is ideal for aiding map-side joins as due to the same value data present in buckets, Merge Sort will be much faster and more efficient. It can be used with or without partitioning.

Summary

In this chapter, we have explored two wrappers of MapReduce programming–Pig and Hive.

MapReduce is very powerful but a very complex high learning curve. The difficult part is to manage the MapReduce programs and the time taken for the development and optimizations. For easier and faster development in MapReduce, we have abstraction layers such as Pig, which is a wrapper of the Pig Latin procedural language on top of MapReduce, and Hive which is a SQL-like HiveQL wrapper.

Pig is used in the data flow model, as it uses the DAG model to transform the Pig Latin language to the MapReduce job. Pig does the transformation in three plans, namely Logical to Physical to MapReduce, where each plan translates the statements and produces an optimized plan of execution. Pig also has the grunt mode for analyzing data interactively. Pig has very useful commands to filter, group, aggregate, cogroup, and so on, and it also supports user-defined functions.

Hive is used by users who are more comfortable in SQL-like development as it has HiveQL. The Hive architecture contains Driver, Metastore, Query compiler, Execution engine, and HiveServer. HiveQL has an exhaustive list of built-in functions and commands to analyze the data. Hive has many in-built functions and also supports user-defined functions.

In the next chapter, we will cover one of the most important components to know in Hadoop. It is a non relational distributed database which gives a high throughput and performance; we call it as HBase.

5
Storage Component – HBase

One of the most important components of the Hadoop ecosystem is HBase, which utilizes HDFS very efficiently and can store, manage, and process data at a much better performing scale. NoSQL is emerging, and there is a lot of attention towards different implementations and solutions in Big Data problem solving space. HBase is a NoSQL database which can process the data over and above HDFS to achieve very good performance with optimization, scalability, and manageability. In Hadoop, HDFS is very good as storage for the WORM (Write Once Read Many) paradigm where data is not updated. In many scenarios, the requirements would be updating, ad hoc analysis or random reads. In HDFS, processing these requirements is not very efficient as updating a record in a file is not possible; HDFS has to delete and rewrite the whole file which is resource, memory and I/O intensive. But HBase can manage such processing efficiently in a huge volume of random read and writes with a near optimal performance.

In this chapter, we will cover the needs and the necessity of HBase and its features, architecture, and design. We will also delve into the data models and schema design, the components of HBase, the read and write pipeline, and some examples.

An Overview of HBase

HBase is designed based on a Google white paper, *Big Table: A Distributed Storage System for Structured Data* and defined as a sparse, distributed, persistent multidimensional sorted map. HBase is a columnar and partition oriented database, but is stored in key value pair of data. I know it's confusing and tricky, so let's look at the terms again in detail.

- **Sparse**: HBase is columnar and partition oriented. Usually, a record may have many columns and many of them may have null data, or the values may be repeated. HBase can efficiently and effectively save the space in sparse data.

- **Distributed**: Data is stored in multiple nodes, scattered across the cluster.
- **Persistent**: Data is written and saved in the cluster.
- **Multidimensional**: A row can have multiple versions or timestamps of values.
- **Map**: Key-Value Pair links the data structure to store the data.
- **Sorted**: The Key in the structure is stored in a sorted order for faster read and write optimization.

The HBase Data Model, as we will see, is very flexible and can be tuned for many Big Data use cases. As with every technology, HBase performs very well in some use cases, but may not be advised in others. The following are the cases where HBase performs well:

- Need of real-time random read/write on a high scale
- Variable Schema: columns can be added or removed at runtime
- Many columns of the datasets are sparse
- Key based retrieval and auto sharding is required
- Need of consistency more than availability
- Data or tables have to be denormalized for better performance

Advantages of HBase

HBase has good number of benefits and is a good solution in many use cases. Let us check some of the advantages of HBase:

- Random and consistent Reads/Writes access in high volume request
- Auto failover and reliability
- Flexible, column-based multidimensional map structure
- Variable Schema: columns can be added and removed dynamically
- Integration with Java client, Thrift and REST APIs
- MapReduce and Hive/Pig integration
- Auto Partitioning and sharding
- Low latency access to data
- BlockCache and Bloom filters for query optimization
- HBase allows data compression and is ideal for sparse data

The Architecture of HBase

HBase is column-oriented by design, where HBase tables are stored in ColumnFamilies and each ColumnFamily can have multiple columns. A ColumnFamily's data are stored in multiple files in multiple Regions where a Region holds the data for a particular range of row keys. To manage Regions, MasterServer assigns multiple Regions to a RegionServer. The flexibility in the design of HBase is due to the flexible RegionServers and Regions, and is controlled by a single MasterServer. HBase Architecture uses Zookeeper to manage the coordination and resource management aspects which are needed to be highly available in a distributed environment. Data management in HBase is efficiently carried out by the splitting and compaction processes carried out in Regions to optimize the data for high volume reading and writing. For processing a high volume of write requests, we have two levels of Cache WAL in RegionServer and MemStore in Regions. If the data for a particular range or row key present in a Region grows larger than the threshold, then the Regions are split to utilize the cluster. Data is merged and compacted using the compaction process. Data recovery is managed using WAL as it holds all the non-persistent edit data.

The HBase architecture emphasizes on scalable concurrent reads and consistent writes. The key to designing an HBase is based on providing high performing and scalable reads and consistent multiple writes. HBase uses the following components which we will discuss later:

- MasterServer
- RegionServer
- Region
- Zookeeper

Lets have a look at the following figure:

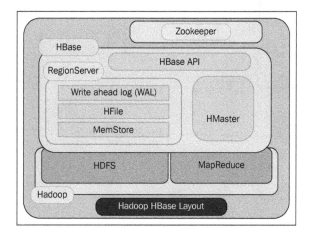

MasterServer

MasterServer is the administrator and at a point of time, there can be only one Master in HBase. It is responsible for the following:

- Cluster monitoring and management
- Assigning Regions to RegionServers
- Failover and load balancing by re-assigning the Regions

RegionServer

RegionServers are identified by the MasterServer, which assigns Regions to a RegionServer. RegionServer runs on a DataNode and performs the following activities:

- Managing the Regions in coordination with the master
- Data splitting in the Regions
- Coordinating and serving the read/write

Along with managing the Regions, RegionServer has the following components or data structures:

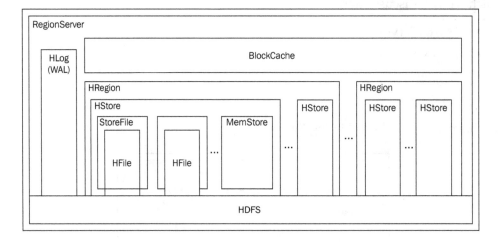

WAL

The data for Write in HBase is first kept in WAL and then put in MemStore. MemStore doesn't persist the data, so if a Region becomes unavailable, the data could get lost. WAL is extremely important in case of any crash, or to recover the data present in the MemStore of a Region which is not responding. WAL holds all the data present in the MemStore of the Regions managed by the RegionServer. When the data is flushed from MemStore and persisted as HFile, the data is removed from WAL too. The acknowledgement of a successful Write is given to the client, only after the data is written in WAL successfully.

BlockCache

HBase caches the data block in BlockCache in each RegionServer when it is read from HDFS for future requests for the block, which optimizes random Reads in HBase. BlockCache works as an in-memory distributed cache. It is an interface and its default implementation is LruBlockCache which is based on the last recently used algorithm cache. In a newer version of HBase, we can use SlabCache and BucketCache implementations. We will discuss all the three implementations in the upcoming sections.

LRUBlockCache

The data blocks are cached in a JVM heap which has three areas based on the access request, that is, single, multi, and in-memory. If a block can be accessed for the first time, then it is saved in single access space. If the block is accessed multiple times, then it is promoted to multi-access. The in-memory area is reserved for blocks loaded from the in-memory flagged column families. The non-frequently accessed blocks are removed using the least recently used technique.

SlabCache

This cache is formed by a combination of the L1(JVM heap) and L2 cache (outside JVM heap). L2 memory is allocated using DirectByteBuffers. The block size can be configured to a higher size as required.

BucketCache

It uses buckets of areas for holding cached blocks. This cache is an extension of SlabCache where, along with the L1 and L2 cache, there is one more level of cache which is of file mode. The file mode is intended for low latency store either in an in-memory filesystem, or in a SSD storage.

 SlabCache or BucketCache are good if the system has to perform at a low latency so that we can utilize the outside JVM heap memory, and when the RAM memory of the RegionServer could be exhausted.

Regions

HBase manages the availability and data distribution with Regions. Regions hold the key for HBase to perform high velocity reads and writes. Regions also manage the row key ordering. It has separate stores per ColumnFamily of the table, and each store has two components MemStore and multiple StoreFiles. HBase achieves auto-sharding using Regions. When the data grows more than the configured maximum size of the store, the files stored in Regions are split into two equal Regions, if auto-splitting is enabled. In a Region, the splitting process maintains the data distribution and the compaction process optimizes the StoreFiles.

A Region can have multiple StoreFiles or blocks that hold the data for HBase, maintained in the HFile format. A StoreFile will hold the data for a ColumnFamily in HBase. ColumnFamily is discussed in the *HBase DataModel* section.

MemStore

MemStore is an in-memory storage space for a Region which holds the data files, called StoreFiles. We have already discussed that data for a write request is first written to WAL of RegionServer, and then it is put into MemStore. One important thing to note is that data is not persistent in MemStore only when the StoreFiles in MemStore reach a threshold value, specifically, the value of the property `hbase.hregion.memstore.flush.size` of `hbase-site.xml` file; the data is flushed as a StoreFile in the Region. As the data has to be in a sorted row key order, it is first written, and then it's sorted before the flush for achieving a faster write. As the data for write is present in MemStore, it also acts as a cache of the data accessed for the recently written block data.

Zookeeper

HBase uses Zookeeper to monitor a RegionServer, and recover it if it is down. All the RegionServers are monitored by ZooKeeper. The RegionServers send heartbeat messages to ZooKeeper, and if within a period of timeout a heartbeat is not received, the RegionServer is considered dead, and the Master starts the recovery process. Zookeeper is also used to identify the active Master and for the election of an active Master.

The HBase data model

Storage of data in HBase is column oriented, in the form of a multi-hierarchical Key-Value map. The HBase Data Model is very flexible and its beauty is to add or remove column data on the fly, without impacting the performance. HBase can be used to process semi-structured data. It doesn't have any specific data types as the data is stored in bytes.

Logical components of a data model

The HBase data model has some logical components which are as follows:

- Tables
- Rows
- Column Families/Columns
- Versions/Timestamp
- Cells

The HBase table is shown in the following figure:

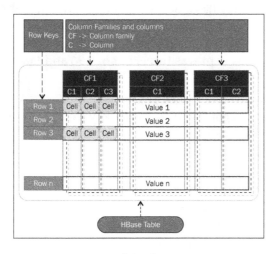

Let's take a look at these components in detail:

- **Tables**: A Table in HBase is actually more logical than physical. An HBase Table can be described as a collection of rows. The data of a Table is presented in different, multiple Regions, and is distributed by the range of rowkey.

- **Rows**: A Row is just a logical representation in HBase. Physically, the data is not stored in row, but in columns. Rows in HBase are combinations of columns which can have multiple column families. Each row in HBase is identified by a rowkey which is used as a primary key index. In a Table, rowkey is unique. If a row to be written has an existing rowkey, then the same row gets updated.

- **Column Families/Columns**: A Column Family is a group of columns which are stored together. Column Families can be used for compression. Designing Column Families is critical for the performance and the utilization of the advantages of HBase. In HBase we store data in denormalization form to create a file which will hold a particular dataset to avoid joins. Ideally, we could have multiple column families in a table but it is not advisable.

  One important thing to note is that it is not advisable for a table in HBase to have more than two level Column Family hierarchies, especially if one family has very high data and other has considerably low data. This is because the smaller sized Column Family data will have to be spread across many Regions and flushing and compaction will not be as efficient as a Region impacts adjacent families too.

  A Column can be accessed in HBase using the column family and a column qualifier is used to access a column's data, for example, `columnfamily:columnname`.

- **Version/Timestamp**: In HBase, a rowkey (row, column, version) holds a cell and we can have the same row and column with a different version to hold multiple cells. HBase stores the versions in descending order of versions so that the recent cell values are found first. Prior to HBase 0.96, the default number of versions kept was three, but in 0.96 and later, it has been changed to one.

- **Cell**: A cell is where the values are written in HBase. A cell in HBase can be defined by a combination of rowkey {row, column, version} in an HBase Table. The data type will be byte[] and the data stored is called value in HBase.

We can represent the relation of HBase components in the following manner:

(Table, RowKey, ColumnFamily, Column, Timestamp) → *Value*

ACID properties

HBase does not follow all the attributes of ACID properties. Let's see here how HBase does adhere to specific properties:

- Atomicity: An operation in HBase either completes entirely or not at all for a row, but across nodes it is eventually consistent.

- Durability: An update in HBase will not be lost due to WAL and MemStore.

- Consistency and Isolation HBase is strongly consistent for a single row level but not across levels.

For more details you can check the site `http://hbase.apache.org/acid-semantics.html`.

The CAP theorem

CAP theorem is also known as Brewer's theorem. CAP stands for:

- Consistency
- Availability
- Partition tolerance

These are the key design properties of any distributed system. We will not get into the details of CAP theorem here but in short, as per the CAP theorem, a distributed system can guarantee only two of the above three properties. As the system is distributed, it has to be Partition tolerant. This leads to two possibilities; either CP, or AP.

HBase has a master-slave architecture. The MasterServer process is single point of failure (we can configure High Availability for the Master which can have a backup Master readily available) while for the RegionServer, recovery from failure is possible but data may be unavailable for some period of time. HBase is actually considered eventually consistent (strongly row level consistent and not strong across levels), and implements consistency and partition tolerance. Hence, HBase is more towards CP than AP.

The Schema design

HBase schema is drastically different from RDBMS schema design as the requirement and the constraints are different. HBase schema should be designed as required by the application and the schema is recommended to be de-normalized. Data distribution depends on the rowkey, which is selected to be uniform across the cluster. Rowkey also has a good impact on the scan performance of the request.

Things to take care of in HBase schema design are as follows:

- **Hotspotting**: Hotspotting is when one or a few Regions have a huge load of data and the data range is frequently written or accessed causing performance degradation. To prevent hotspotting, we can hash a value of rowkey or a particular column so that the probability of uniform distribution is high and the read and write will be optimized.

- **Monotonically increasing Rowkeys/Timeseries data**: A problem arising with multiple Regions is that a range of rowkeys could reach the threshold of splitting and can lead to a period of timeout. To avoid this, we should not have the increasing column value as the initial value of rowkey.

- **Reverse Timestamp**: If we have timestamp in rowkey, the newer data is pushed at the end. If the timestamp is stored like `Long.MAX_VALUE` timestamp, then the newer data will be present at the start and will be faster and can be avoided, especially in case of a scan.

Let's look at some important concepts for designing schema in HBase:

- **Rowkey**: Rowkey is an extremely important design parameter in HBase schema as the data is indexed using rowkey. Rowkey is immutable; the only way to change a rowkey is to delete and re-insert it again. Rows are sorted by **Rowkeylexicographically**, that is, if the rowkey is `1, 32, 001, 225, 060, 45` the order in which the numbers will be sorted would be `001, 060, 1, 225, 32, 45`. Table files are distributed across Regions by a range of Rowkey. Usually a combination of sequential and random keys performs better in HBase.

- **Column Families**: Column Family provides good scalability and flexibility but should be designed carefully. In the current architecture of HBase, no more than two Column Families are advised.

- **Denormalize data**: As HBase doesn't provide Joins on its own, data should be denormalized. The data will usually be sparse and repeated in many columns, which HBase can take full advantage of.

The Write pipeline

Write pipeline in HBase is carried out by the following steps:

1. Client requests data to be written in HTable, the request comes to a RegionServer.

2. The RegionServer writes the data first in WAL.

3. The RegionServer identifies the Region which will store the data and the data will be saved in MemStore of that Region.

4. MemStore holds the data in memory and does not persist it. When the threshold value reaches in the MemStore, then the data is flushed as a HFile in that region.

The Read pipeline

Read in HBase is performed in the following steps:

1. Client sends a read request. The request is received by the RegionServer which identifies all the Regions where the HFiles are present.

2. First, the MemStore of the Region is queried; if the data is present, then the request is serviced.

3. If the data is not present, the BlockCache is queried to check if it has the data; if yes, the request is serviced.

4. If the data is not present in the BlockCache, then it is pulled from the Region and serviced. Now the data is cached in MemStore and BlockCache..

Compaction

In HBase, the MemStore in Regions creates many HFiles for a Column Family. This large number of files will require more time to read and hence, can impact the read performance. To improve the performance, HBase performs compaction to merge files in order to reduce their number and to keep the data manageable. The compaction process identifies the StoreFiles to merge by running an algorithm which is called compaction policy. There are two types of compactions: minor compactions and major compactions.

The Compaction policy

Compaction policy is the algorithm which can be used to select the StoreFiles for merging. Two policies are possible and the available ones are `ExploringCompactionPolicy` and `RatioBasedCompactionPolicy`. To set the policy algorithm, we have to set the value of the property `hbase.hstore.defaultengine.compactionpolicy.class` of `hbase-site.xml`. RatioBasedCompactionPolicy was available as the default policy prior to HBase 0.96 and is still available. ExploringCompactionPolicy is the default algorithm from HBase 0.96 and the later version. The difference in these algorithms, in short, is that the RatioBasedCompactionPolicy selects the first set that matches the criteria while the ExploringCompactionPolicy selects the best possible set of StoreFiles with the least work and is better suited for bulk loading of data.

Minor compaction

Minor compaction merges or rewrites adjacent and smaller sized StoreFiles into one StoreFile. Minor compaction will be faster as it creates a new StoreFile and the StoreFiles selected for Compaction are immutable. Please note that Minor compaction does not handle the deleted and expired versions. It occurs when a number of StoreFiles reach a threshold value; to be very specific, the value of the `hbase.hstore.compaction.min` property in the `hbase-site.xml`. The default value of the property is 2 and Minor compaction simply merges the smaller file to reduce the number of files. This will be faster as data is already sorted. Some more configurable properties that influence Minor compaction are as follows:

- `hbase.store.compaction.ratio`: This value determines the balance between the read cost and write cost, a higher value will have a very less number of files having a high read speed and a high write cost. A lesser value will have a lower write cost while the read cost will be comparatively higher. The value recommended is between 1.0 to 1.4.

- `hbase.hstore.compaction.min.size`: This value indicates the minimum size below which the StoreFiles will be included for compaction. The default value is 128 MB.

- `hbase.hstore.compaction.max.size`: This value indicates the maximum size above which the StoreFiles will not be included for compaction. The default value is `Long.MAX_VALUE`.

- `hbase.hstore.compaction.min`: This value indicates the minimum number of files below which the StoreFiles will be included for compaction. The default value is 2.

- `hbase.hstore.compaction.max.size`: This value indicates the maximum number of files above which the StoreFiles will not be included for compaction. The default value is 10.

Major compaction

Major compaction consolidates all the StoreFiles of a Region into one StoreFile. The Major Compaction process takes a lot of time as it actually removes the expired versions and deleted data. The initiation of this process can be time triggered, manual, and size triggered. By default, Major Compaction runs every 24 hours but it is recommended to start it manually as it is a write intensive and a resource intensive process, and can block write requests to prevent JVM heap exhaustion. The configurable properties impacting Major Compaction are:

- `hbase.hregion.majorcompaction`: This denotes the time, in milliseconds, between two Major compactions. We can disable time triggered Major compaction by setting the value of this property to 0. The default value is 604800000 milliseconds (7 days).

- `hbase.hregion.majorcompaction.jitter`: The actual time of Major Compaction is calculated by this property value and multiplied by the above property hbase.hregion.majorcompaction value. The smaller the value, the more frequent the compaction will start. The default value is 0.5 f.

Splitting

As we discussed about the file and data management in HBase, along with compaction, Splitting Regions also is an important process. The best performance in HBase is achieved when the data is distributed evenly across the Regions and RegionServers which can be achieved by Splitting the Region optimally. When a table is first created with default options, only one Region is allocated to the table as HBase will not have sufficient information to allocate the appropriate number of Regions. We have three types of Splitting triggers which are Pre-Splitting, Auto Splitting, and Forced Splitting.

Pre-Splitting

To aid the splitting of a Region while creating a table, we can use Pre-Splitting to let HBase know initially the number of Regions to allocate to a table. For Pre-Splitting we should know the distribution of the data and if we Pre-Split the Regions and we have a data skew, then the distribution will be non-uniform and can limit the cluster performance. We also have to calculate the split points for the table which can be done using the RegionSplitter utility. RegionSplitter uses pluggable SplitAlgorithm and two pre-defined algorithms available which are HexStringSplit and UniformSplit. HexStringSplit can be used if the row keys have prefix for hexadecimal strings and UniformSplit can be used assuming they are random byte arrays, or we can implement and use our own custom SplitAlgorithm.

The following is an example of using Pre-Splitting:

```
$ hbase org.apache.hadoop.hbase.util.RegionSplitter
  pre_splitted_table HexStringSplit -c 10 -f f1
```

In this command, we use the RegionSplitter with table name `pre_splitted_table`, with `SplitAlgorithm HexStringSplit` and `10` number of regions and `f1` is the ColumnFamily name. It creates a table called, `pre_splitted_table` with 10 regions.

Auto Splitting

HBase performs Auto Splitting when a Region size increases above a threshold value, to be very precise, value of property `hbase.hregion.max.filesize` of `hbase-site.xml` file which has a default value of 10 GB.

Forced Splitting

In many cases, the data distribution can be non-uniform after the data increases. HBase allows the user to split all Regions of a table or a particular Region by specifying a split key. The command to trigger Forced Splitting is as follows:

```
split 'tableName'
split 'tableName', 'splitKey'
split 'regionName', 'splitKey'
```

Commands

To enter in HBase shell mode, use the following:

```
$ ${HBASE_HOME}/bin/hbase shell
.

.

HBase Shell;
hbase>
```

You can use `help` to get a list of all commands.

help

```
hbase> help
HBASE SHELL COMMANDS:
```

Create

Used for creating a new table in HBase. For now we will stick to the simplest version which is as follows:

```
hbase> create 'test', 'cf'
0 row(s) in 1.2200 seconds
```

List

Use the `list` command to display the list of tables created, which is as follows:

```
hbase> list 'test'
TABLE
test
1 row(s) in 0.0350 seconds


=> ["test"]
```

Put

To put data into your table, use the `put` command:

```
hbase> put 'test', 'row1', 'cf:a', 'value1'
0 row(s) in 0.1770 seconds


hbase> put 'test', 'row2', 'cf:b', 'value2'
0 row(s) in 0.0160 seconds
hbase> put 'test', 'row3', 'cf:c', 'value3'
0 row(s) in 0.0260 seconds
```

Scan

The `Scan` command is used to scan the table for data. You can limit your scan, but for now, all data is fetched:

```
hbase> scan 'test'
ROW          COLUMN+CELL
 row1        column=cf:a, timestamp=1403759475114, value=value1
 row2        column=cf:b, timestamp=1403759492807, value=value2
 row3        column=cf:c, timestamp=1403759503155, value=value3
3 row(s) in 0.0440 seconds
```

Get

The `Get` command will retrieve a single row of data at a time, which is shown in the following command:

```
hbase> get 'test', 'row1'
COLUMN                  CELL
```

```
 cf:a                    timestamp=1403759475114, value=value1
1 row(s) in 0.0230 seconds
```

Disable

To make any setting changes in a table, we have to disable a table using the `disable` command, perform the action, and re-enable it. You can re-enable it using the `enable` command. The disable command is explained in the following command:

```
hbase> disable 'test'
0 row(s) in 1.6270 seconds


hbase> enable 'test'
0 row(s) in 0.4500 seconds
```

Drop

The `Drop` command drops or deletes a table, which is shown as follows:

```
hbase> drop 'test'
0 row(s) in 0.2900 seconds
```

HBase Hive integration

Analysts usually prefer a Hive environment due to the comfort of SQL-like syntax. HBase is well integrated with Hive, using the StorageHandler that Hive interfaces with. The create table syntax in Hive will look like the following:

```
CREATE EXTERNAL TABLE hbase_table_1(key int, value string)
STORED BY 'org.apache.hadoop.hive.hbase.HBaseStorageHandler'
WITH SERDEPROPERTIES ("hbase.columns.mapping" =
":key,ColumnFamily:Column1, columnFalimy:column2")
TBLPROPERTIES ("hbase.table.name" = "xyz");
```

Let us understand the syntax and the keywords used for the table:

- `EXTERNAL`: This is used if the table in HBase exists already, or if the table in HBase is new and you want Hive to manage only the metadata and not the actual data.

- `STORED BY`: The HBaseStorageHandler has to be used to handle the input and output from HBase.

- **SERDEPROPERTIES**: Hive column to HBase ColumnFamily:Column mapping has to be specified here. In this example, key maps as a rowkey and value maps to val column of ColumnFamily cf1.

- **TBLPROPERTIES**: Maps the HBase table name.

Performance tuning

The HBase architecture provides the flexibility of using different optimizations to help the system perform optimally, increase the scalability and efficiency, and provide better performance. HBase is the most popular NoSQL technology due to its flexible Data Model and its interface components.

The components that are very useful and widely used are:

- Compression
- Filters
- Counters
- HBase co-processors

Compression

HBase can utilize compression due to its column-oriented design which is ideal for block compression on Column Families. HBase handles sparse data in an optimal way as no reference or space is occupied for null values. Compressions can be of different types and can be compared depending upon the compression ratio, encoding time, and decoding time. By default, HBase doesn't apply or enable any Compression; for using Compression, the Column Family has to be enabled.

Some compression types which are available to plugin are as follows:

- **GZip**: It provides a higher compression ratio, but encoding and decoding is slow and space intensive. We can use GZip as compression for infrequent data which needs high compression ratio.

- **LZO**: It provides faster encoding and decoding, but a lower compression ratio compared to GZip. LZO is under GPL license, hence it's, not shipped along with HBase.

- **Snappy**: Snappy is the ideal compression type and provides faster encoding or decoding. Its compression ratio lies somewhere between that of LZO and GZip. Snappy is under BSD license by Google.

The code for enabling Compression on a ColumnFamily of an Existing Table using HBase Shell is as follows:

```
hbase> disable 'test'
hbase> alter 'test', {NAME => 'cf', COMPRESSION => 'GZ'}
hbase> enable 'test'
```

For creating a new table with compression on a ColumnFamily, the code is as follows:

```
hbase> create 'test2', { NAME => 'cf2', COMPRESSION => 'SNAPPY' }
```

Filters

Filters in HBase can be used to filter data according to some condition. They are very useful for reducing the volume of data to be processed, and especially helps save the network bandwidth and the amount of data to process for the client. Filters move the processing logic towards data in the nodes and the result is accumulated and sent to the client. This enhances the performance with a manageable process and code. Filters are powerful enough to be processed for a row, column, Column Family, Qualifier, Value, Timestamp, and so on. Filters are preferred to be used as a Java API, but can also be used from an HBase shell. Filters can be used to perform some ad hoc analysis as well.

Some frequently used filters, like those listed next, are already available and are quite useful:

- **Column Value**: The most widely used Filter types are Column Value as HBase has a column-oriented architectural design. We will now take a look at some popular Column Value oriented filters:

- **SingleColumnValueFilter**: A SingleColumnValueFilter filters the data on a column value of an HBase table.

  ```
  Syntax:
  SingleColumnValueFilter ('<ColumnFamily>', '<qualifier>', <compare
  operator>, '<comparator>'
  [, <filterIfColumnMissing_boolean>] [, <latest_version_boolean>])


  Usage:
  SingleColumnValueFilter ('ColFamilyA', 'Column1', <=, 'abc', true,
  false)
  SingleColumnValueFilter ('ColFamilyA', 'Column1', <=, 'abc')
  ```

- **SingleColumnValueExcludeFilter**: the SingleColumnValueExcludeFilter is useful to exclude values from a column value of an HBase table.

  ```
  Syntax:
  SingleColumnValueExcludeFilter (<ColumnFamily>, <qualifier>,
    <compare operators>, <comparator> [,
      <latest_version_boolean>] [,
        <filterIfColumnMissing_boolean>])
  ```

  ```
  Example:
  SingleColumnValueExcludeFilter ('FamilyA', 'Column1', '<=',
    'abc', 'false', 'true')
  SingleColumnValueExcludeFilter ('FamilyA', 'Column1', '<=',
    'abc')
  ```

- **ColumnRangeFilter**: The ColumnRangeFilter operates on the Column for filtering the column based on minColumn, maxColumn, or both. We can either enable or disable the minColumnValue constraint by `minColumnInclusive_bool` Boolean parameter, and `maxColumnValue` by `maxColumnInclusive_bool`.

  ```
  Syntax:
  ColumnRangeFilter ('<minColumn >', <minColumnInclusive_bool>,
  '<maxColumn>', <maxColumnInclusive_bool>)
  ```

  ```
  Example:
  ColumnRangeFilter ('abc', true, 'xyz', false)
  ```

- **KeyValue**: Some filters operate on Key-Value data.

- **FamilyFilter**: It operates on Column Family and compares each family name with the comparator; it returns all the key-values in that family if the comparison returns true.

  ```
  Syntax:
  FamilyFilter (<compareOp>, '<family_comparator>')
  ```

- **QualifierFilter**: It operates on the qualifier and compares each qualifier name with the comparator.

  ```
  Syntax:
  QualifierFilter (<compareOp>, '<qualifier_comparator>')
  ```

- **RowKey**: Filters can also work on row level comparison and filter data.

- **RowFilter**: Compares each row key with the comparator using the compare operator.

  ```
  Syntax:
  RowFilter (<compareOp>, '<row_comparator>')
  ```

```
Example:
RowFilter (<=, 'binary:xyz)
```

- **Multiple Filters**: We can add a combination of Filters to a FilterList and scan them. We can choose to have OR, or AND between the filters by using:

```
FilterList.Operator.MUST_PASS_ALL or
  FilterList.Operator.MUST_PASS_ONE.
```

```
FilterList list = new
  FilterList(FilterList.Operator.MUST_PASS_ONE);
```

```
// Use some filter and add it in the list.
```

```
list.add(filter1);
```

```
scan.setFilter(list);
```

We have many other useful filters which are available and if we need, then we can also create a custom based filter.

Counters

Another useful feature of HBase is Counters. They can be used as a distributed Counter to increment a column value, without the overhead of locking the complete row and reducing the synchronization on Write, for incrementing a value. Incrementing or counters are required in many scenarios, especially in many analytical systems like digital marketing, click stream analysis, document index models, and so on. HBase Counters can manage with very less overhead. Distributed Counter is very useful but poses different challenges in a distributed environment as the counter values will be present in multiple servers at the same time and the write and read requests will be considerably high. Therefore, to be efficient, we have two types of Counters present in HBase which are single and multiple counters. Multiple counters can be designed to count in an individual hierarchical level according to rowkey distribution and can be used by summing up the Counters to get the whole counter value. The types of counter are explained as follows:

- **Single Counter**: Single Counters work on specified columns in the HTable, row wise. The methods for Single Counters provided for an HTable, are as follows:

```
long incrementColumnValue(byte[] row, byte[] family, byte[]
  qualifier,long amount) throws IOException
long incrementColumnValue(byte[] row, byte[] family, byte[]
  qualifier,long amount, boolean writeToWAL) throws
    IOException
```

We should use the second method with `writeToWAL` to specify whether the write-ahead log should be active or not.

- **Multiple Counter**: Multiple Counters will work qualifier-wise in the HTable. The method for Multiple Counters provided for an HTable is as follows:

```
Increment addColumn(byte[] family, byte[] qualifier, long
    amount)
```

HBase coprocessors

Coprocessor is a framework which HBase provides to empower and execute some custom code on RegionServers. Coprocessors move the computation much closer to the data, specifically Region-wise. Coprocessors are quite useful for calculating aggregators, secondary indexing, complex filtering, auditing, and authorization.

HBase has some useful coprocessors implemented and open for the extension and custom implementation of a Coprocessor. Coprocessors can be designed based on two strategies- Observer and Endpoint, which are as follows:

- **Observer**: As the name suggests, Observer coprocessors can be designed to work as a callback or in case of some event. Observers can be thought of as triggers in RDBMS and can be operated at Region, Master, or WAL levels. Observers have the `PreXXX` and `PostXXX` conventions for methods to override, before and after an event respectively. The following are the types of Observer according to the different levels:

  ○ **RegionObserver**: The Region Observers process Region level data. These can be used for creating secondary indexes to aid retrieval. For every HTable Region, we can have a RegionObserver. RegionObserver provides hooks for data manipulation events, such as `Get`, `Put`, `Delete`, `Scan`, and so on. Common example include `preGet` and `postGet` for `Get` operation and `prePut` and `postPut` for `Put` operation.

  ○ **MasterObserver**: The MasterObserver operates at the Master Level where the DDL-type operations like create, delete, and modify table are processed. Extreme care should be taken to utilize MasterObserver.

  ○ **WALObserver**: This provides hooks around the WAL processing. It has only two methods; `preWALWrite()` and `postWALWrite()`.

- **Endpoint**: Endpoints are operations which can be called via a client interface by directly invoking it. If Observers can be thought of as triggers, then Endpoint can be thought of as Stored Procedures of RDBMS. HBase can have tens of millions of rows or many more; if we need to compute an aggregate function, like a sum on that HTable, we can write an Endpoint coprocessor which will be executed within the Regions and will return the computed result from a Region as in map side processing. Later from all Regions result can perform the sum as in reduce side processing. The advantage of Endpoint is that the processing will be closer to the data and the integration will be much more efficient.

Summary

In this chapter, you have learned that HBase is a NoSQL, Column-oriented database with flexible schema. It has the following components – MasterServer, RegionServer, and Regions and utilizes Zookeeper to monitor them with two caches – WAL in RegionServers and MemStore in Regions. We also saw how HBase manages the data by performing RegionSplitting and Compaction. HBase provides partition tolerance and much higher consistency levels as compared to availability from the CAP theorem.

The HBase Data Model is different from the traditional RDBMS as data is stored in a column oriented database and in a multidimensional map of key-value pairs. Rows are identified by rowkey and are distributed across clusters using a range of values of rowkey. Rowkey is critical in designing schema for HBase for performance and data management.

In a Hadoop project, data management is a very critical step. In the context of Big Data, Hadoop has the benefit of the data management aspect. But managing it with some scripts becomes difficult and poses many challenges. We will cover these in the next chapter with tools that can help us in managing the data with Sqoop and Flume.

6
Data Ingestion in Hadoop – Sqoop and Flume

Data ingestion is critical and should be emphasized for any big data project, as the volume of data is usually in terabytes or petabytes, maybe exabytes. Handling huge amounts of data is always a challenge and critical. As big data systems are popular to process unstructured or semi-structured data, this brings in complex and many data sources that have huge amount of data. With each data source, the complexity of system increases. Many domains or data types such as social media, marketing, genes in healthcare, video and audio systems, telecom CDR, and so on have diverse sources of data. Many of these produce or send data consistently on a large scale. The key issue is to manage the data consistency and how to leverage the resource available. Data ingestion, in particular, is complex in Hadoop or generally big data as data sources and processing are now in batch, stream, real-time. This also increases the complexity and management.

In this chapter, we will look at some of the challenges in data ingestion in Hadoop and possible solutions of using tools like Sqoop and Flume. We will cover Sqoop and Flume in detail.

Data sources

Due to the capability of processing variety of data and volume of data, data sources for Hadoop has increased and along with that the complexity has increased enormously. We now see huge amount of batch and streaming and real-time analysis processed in Hadoop, for which data ingestion can become a bottleneck or can break a system, if not designed according to the requirement.

Let's look at some of the data sources, which can produce enormous volume of data or consistent data continuously:

- **Data sensors**: These are thousands of sensors, producing data continuously.
- **Machine Data**: Produces data which should be processed in near real time for avoiding huge loss.
- **Telco Data**: CDR data and other telecom data generates high volume of data.
- **Healthcare system data**: Genes, images, ECR records are unstructured and complex to process.
- **Social Media**: Facebook, Twitter, Google Plus, YouTube, and others get a huge volume of data.
- **Geological Data**: Semiconductors and other geological data produce huge volumes of data.
- **Maps**: Maps have a huge volume of data, and processing data is also a challenge in Maps.
- **Aerospace**: Flight details and runway management systems produce high-volume data and processing in real time.
- **Astronomy**: Planets and other objects produce heavy images, which have to be processed at a faster rate.
- **Mobile Data**: Mobile generates many events and a huge volume of data at a high velocity rate.

These are just some domains or data sources that produce data in Terabytes or Exabytes. Data ingestion is critical and can make or break a system.

Challenges in data ingestion

The following are the challenges in data source ingestion:

- Multiple source ingestion
- Streaming / real-time ingestion
- Scalability
- Parallel processing
- Data quality
- Machine data can be on a high scale in GB per minute

Sqoop

Sqoop can process data transfer between traditional databases, Hadoop, and NoSQL database like HBase and Cassandra efficiently. Sqoop helps by providing a utility to import and export data in Hadoop from these data sources. Sqoop helps in executing the process in parallel and therefore in much faster speed. Sqoop utilizes connectors and drivers to connect with the underlying database source, and executes the import and export in multiple Mapper process, in order to execute the data in parallel and faster. Sqoop can process bulk data transfers on HDFS, Hive, or HBase.

Connectors and drivers

Sqoop utility needs drivers and connectors for data transfer between a database and Hadoop. One of the important step in configuring Sqoop is to get the driver and configure it with Sqoop. Drivers are required by Sqoop to connect with them and should be the JDBC drivers for Sqoop 1 that are provided by the database vendor for the respective database. Drivers are not shipped with Sqoop as some drivers are licensed, hence we have to get the JDBC driver of the database and keep it in the Sqoop library. Connectors are required to optimize the data transfer by getting metadata information of the database. All RDBMS Databases use SQL, but some commands and syntax vary with other databases. This makes it difficult to get the metadata and optimize the data. Sqoop provides generic connectors that will work with databases such as MySQL, Oracle, PostgreSQL, DB2, and SQL Server, but are not optimal. For optimal performance, some vendors have released their connectors that can be plugged with Sqoop, which is shown in the following figure:

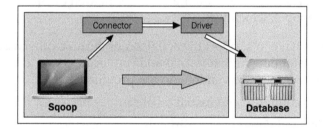

Sqoop 1 architecture

Sqoop1 architecture is a client-side tool, which is tightly coupled with the Hadoop cluster. A Sqoop command initiated by the client fetches the metadata of the tables, columns, and data types, according to the connectors and drivers interfaces. The import or export is translated to a Map-only Job program to load the data in parallel between the databases and Hadoop. Clients should have the appropriate connector and driver for the execution of the process.

The Sqoop architecture is shown in the following figure:

Limitation of Sqoop 1

Few limitations that were realized after a wide adaptation of Sqoop 1 for data ingestion led to Sqoop 2, which were:

- Connectors have to support the serialization format, otherwise Sqoop cannot transfer data in that format and connectors have to be JDBC drivers. Some database vendors do not provide it.
- Not easy to configure and install.
- Monitoring and debugging is difficult.
- Security concerns as Sqoop 1 requires root access to install and configure it.
- Only the command line argument is supported.
- Connectors are only JDBC-based.

Sqoop 2 architecture

Sqoop 2 architecture overcomes the limitations of Sqoop 1, which we discussed earlier. The features of Sqoop 2 are:

- Sqoop 2 exposes REST API as a web service, which can be easily integrated with other systems.

- The connectors and drivers are managed centrally in one place.

- Sqoop 2 is well configured and integrated with HBase, Hive, and Oozie for interoperability and management.

- Connectors can be non-JDBC based.

- As a service-oriented design, Sqoop 2 can have role-based authentication and audit trail logging to increase the security.

The following is an architecture of Sqoop 2:

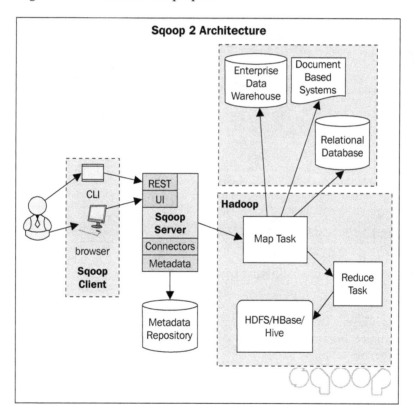

Imports

Sqoop import is executed in two steps:

1. Gather metadata
2. Submit map only job

The following figure explains the import in to Sqoop:

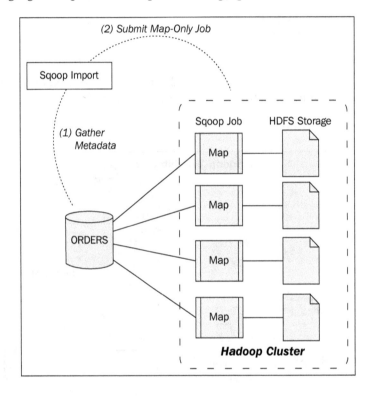

Sqoop import provides the following options:

- Import an entire table:

```
sqoop import \
--connect jdbc:mysql://mysql.example.com/sqoop \
--username sqoop \
--password sqoop \
--table cities
```

- Import a subset of data:

```
sqoop import \
--connect jdbc:mysql://mysql.example.com/sqoop \
--username sqoop \
--password sqoop \
--table cities \
--where "country = 'USA'"
```

- Change file format, by default the data will be saved in tab separated csv format but Sqoop provides option for saving the data in Hadoop SequenceFile, Avro binary format and Parquet file:

```
sqoop import \
--connect jdbc:mysql://mysql.example.com/sqoop \
--username sqoop \
--password sqoop \
--table cities \
--as-sequencefile

sqoop import \
--connect jdbc:mysql://mysql.example.com/sqoop \
--username sqoop \
--password sqoop \
--table cities \
--as-avrodatafile
```

- Compressing imported data:

```
sqoop import \
--connect jdbc:mysql://mysql.example.com/sqoop \
--username sqoop \
--table cities \
--compress \
--compression-codec org.apache.hadoop.io.compress.BZip2Codec
```

- Bulk import:

```
sqoop import \
--connect jdbc:mysql://mysql.example.com/sqoop \
--username sqoop \
--table cities \
--direct
```

- Importing all your table:

```
sqoop import-all-tables \
--connect jdbc:mysql://mysql.example.com/sqoop \
--username sqoop \
--password sqoop
```

- Incremental import:

```
sqoop import \
--connect jdbc:mysql://mysql.example.com/sqoop \
--username sqoop \
--password sqoop \
--table visits \
--incremental append \
--check-column id \
--last-value 1
```

- Free form query import:

```
sqoop import \
--connect jdbc:mysql://mysql.example.com/sqoop \
--username sqoop \
--password sqoop \
--query 'SELECT normcities.id, \
    countries.country, \
    normcities.city \
    FROM normcities \
    JOIN countries USING(country_id) \
    WHERE $CONDITIONS' \
--split-by id \
--target-dir cities
```

- Custom boundary query import:

```
sqoop import \
--connect jdbc:mysql://mysql.example.com/sqoop \
--username sqoop \
--password sqoop \
--query 'SELECT normcities.id, \
countries.country, \
normcities.city \
FROM normcities \
JOIN countries USING(country_id) \
WHERE $CONDITIONS' \
--split-by id \
--target-dir cities \
--boundary-query "select min(id), max(id) from normcities"
```

Exports

Sqoop Export is also in a similar process, only the source will be HDFS. Export is performed in two steps;

- Gather metadata
- Submit map-only job

The following figure explains the export into Sqoop:

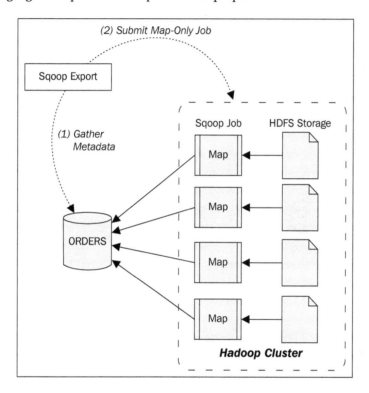

Sqoop Export has following options:

- Exporting files from under the HDFS directory to a table:

```
sqoop export \
--connect jdbc:mysql://mysql.example.com/sqoop \
--username sqoop \
--password sqoop \
--table cities \
--export-dir cities
```

- Batch inserts export:

```
sqoop export \
--connect jdbc:mysql://mysql.example.com/sqoop \
--username sqoop \
--password sqoop \
--table cities \
--export-dir cities \
--batch
```

- Updating existing dataset:

```
sqoop export \
--connect jdbc:mysql://mysql.example.com/sqoop \
--username sqoop \
--password sqoop \
--table cities \
--update-key id
```

- Upsert export:

```
sqoop export \
--connect jdbc:mysql://mysql.example.com/sqoop \
--username sqoop \
--password sqoop \
--table cities \
--update-key id \
--update-mode allowinsert
```

- Column export:

```
sqoop export \
--connect jdbc:mysql://mysql.example.com/sqoop \
--username sqoop \
--password sqoop \
--table cities \
--columns country,city
```

Apache Flume

Flume is extremely popular data ingestion system, which can be used to ingest data from different multiple sources and can put it in multiple destinations. Flume provides a framework to handle and process data on a larger scale, and it is very reliable.

Flume is usually described as distributed, reliable, scalable, manageable, and customizable to ingest and process data from different multiple data sources to multiple destinations.

As we already discussed about the different type of data sources. One thing which makes the design more difficult is that data formats changes frequently in some cases especially social media data in JSON, and usually a Big Data systems has multiple data sources. Flume is extremely efficient in handling such scenarios and provides a greater control over each data source and the processing layer. Flume can be configured in three modes: single node, pseudo-distributed, and fully-distributed mode.

Flume is adapted due to its capability to be highly reliable, flexible, customizable, extensible, and can work in a distributed manner in parallel to process big data.

Reliability

Reliability in distributed environment is difficult to design and achieve. Flume excels in the reliability aspect. Flume handles the logical component dynamically to achieve load balancing and reliability. It can guarantee the delivery of the message if the agent node is active. As we mentioned, reliability is difficult to achieve, although Flume can achieve it with some cost and can be resource intensive. According to the requirement and need, Flume provides three levels of reliability, which are:

- **End-to-end**: The end-to-end level is the most reliable level and guarantees the delivery of an event as long as the agent is alive. The durability is achieved by writing the event in a **Write Ahead Log (WAL)** file that can be used to recover the events, even in case of crash.

- **Store on failure**: The store on failure level relies on the confirmation acknowledgement of sending events to sink. In case of acknowledgment not received by the node, the data is stored in the local disk and waits till the node recovers of another node is identified. This level is reliable, but

- can have data loss in case of silent failure.

- **Best effort**: The best effort level is the lowest in reliability and can have data loss, but data processing will be faster. In best effort, no attempt will be made to retry or confirm, hence data can be lost.

Flume architecture

Flume architecture is a very flexible and customizable composed agent that can be configured as multitiered for a data flow process. The data flow design allows the source or data to be transferred or processed from the source to the destination. The components are wired together in chains and in different tiers called the logical node's configuration. The logical nodes are configured in three tiers, namely, Client, Collector, and Storage. The first tier is the Client that captures the data from data source and forwards the it to the Collector, which consolidates the data after processing and sends it to the Storage tier.

The Flume process and the logical components are controlled by the Flume Master. The logical nodes are very flexible and can be added or deleted dynamically by the Master.

Multitier topology

In Flume, Agents can be configured to be a Client, Collector, or Storage. A Client Agent ingests the data from a data source and pushes it to another Agent, using an Avro/Thrift or intermediatory storage area. A Collector Agent takes an input from another Agent and acts as a source for the Storage Agent. A Storage Agent takes an input from a collector Agent or another Agent and saves the data at the end storage location. Each tier can have multiple independent Agents, which can act as a load balancer. Tier Sink can forward the events to any of the available next hop destination. The flume topology is shown in the following figure:

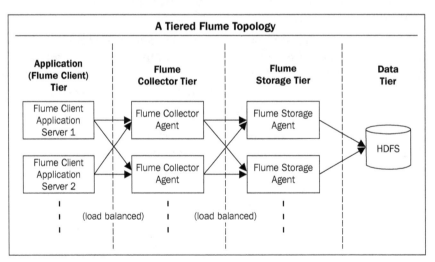

Flume physical has two components: Flume Master and Flume Nodes.

Flume master

Flume Master, as we mentioned earlier, assigns and coordinates the physical and dynamic logical layer, hence, Master is important in achieving the flexibility and reliability. The logical nodes also check with Master for any updates in configuration. For achieving high availability of Master, we can configure multiple Masters or use Zookeeper to manage Master and Nodes.

Flume nodes

Flume Nodes are physical JVM processes, which run in each nodes. In Flume, each machine has a single JVM process as a physical node that acts as a container for multiple logical processes. Even though Agents and the Collectors are logically separate processes, they can run in the same machine.

Logical components in Flume have two components, namely, Event and Agent. We will discuss the following components:

- **Events**: Flume has a data flow model, where a unit of data in the flow is called an Event. Events carry payload and an optional set of headers. Events can be customized by implementing Event Interface or overriding existing Event in Flume. Events flow through one or more Agents specifically from Source to the Channel to the Sink component of Agent.

- **Agent**: An Agent in Flume provides the flexibility to Flume architecture, as it runs on a separate JVM process. An Agent in Flume has three components: Source, Channel, and Sink. Agent works on hop-by-hop flow. It receives events from the Source and puts it in a Channel. It then stores or processes the events and forwards them via Sink to the next hop destination. An Agent can have multiple Sink to forward the events to multiple Agents. The following figure explains the Agent's role:

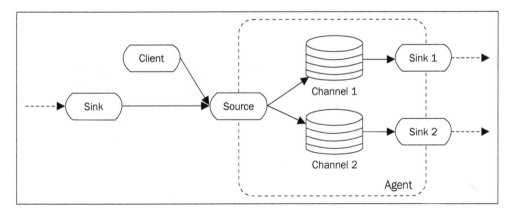

Components in Agent

Let's look at the components of Agent, that is, Source and Sink in the upcoming sections.

Source

Source only listens and receives events from the data source. It then translates it into events and puts it in the Channels Queue. Flume is very well integrated with various source types such as Avro, Thrift, HTTP, and others. For defining a source, we have to set the values of property type. Some frequently used source types are:

Source Type	value of property Type	Mandatory property to set for the source type
Avro	`avro`	bind: hostname or IP address port: Port # to bind to
Thrift	`thrift`	bind: hostname or IP address port: Port # to bind to
Unix command	`exec`	command: unix command to execute like tail or cat
JMS source	`jms`	`initialContextFactory`: Example: `org.apache.activemq.jndi.ActiveMQInitialContextFactory` `connectionFactory`: The JNDI name the connection factory should appear as: `providerURL`: The JMS provider URL `destinationName`; Destination name `destinationType`: Destination type (queue or topic)
Spooling directory source	`spooldir`	`spoolDir`: The directory from which to read files from
Twitter	`org.apache.flume.source.twitter.TwitterSource`	P.S.: This source is highly experimental and may change between minor versions of Flume. Use at your own risk: `consumerKey`: OAuth consumer key `consumerSecret`: OAuth consumer secret `accessToken`: OAuth access token `accessTokenSecret`: OAuth token secret

Source Type	value of property Type	Mandatory property to set for the source type
NetCat source	`netcat`	bind: hostname or IP address port: Port # to bind to
Sequence generator source	`seq`	Sequence generator starts with 0 and incremental by 1 index.
HTTP source	`http`	port: Port # to bind to

For more details, we can check the Apache Flume user guide page `https://flume.apache.org/FlumeUserGuide.html#flume-sources`.

Example: For creating a source of Agent that should get the updated data of a log file, the mandatory parameter and value should be:

- **type**: `exec`
- **command**: `tail -f log_file`
- **channels**: `<channel_name>`

The preceding points are explained in the following command:

```
agent.sources.source_log-tail.type = exec
agent.sources.source_log-tail.command = tail -F /log/system.log
agent.sources.source_log-tail.channels = channel1
```

Sink

Sink collects the events from channels and forwards it to next hop destination as an output of the Agent.

For defining a sink, we have to set values of property type. Some frequently used sink types are:

Sink type	value of property type	Mandatory property to set for the sink type
HDFS sink	`hdfs`	`hdfs.path` – HDFS directory path
Logger sink	`logger`	
Avro	`avro`	bind: hostname or IP address port: Port # to bind to
Thrift	`thrift`	bind: hostname or IP address port: Port # to bind to

Sink type	value of property type	Mandatory property to set for the sink type
IRC sink	`irc`	`hostname`: hostname or IP address `nick`: Nick name `chan`: channel
File Roll Sink	`file_roll`	`sink.directory`: The directory where files will be stored
Null Sink	`null`	
HBaseSinks	`hbase`	`table`: The name of the table in HBase to write to. `columnFamily`: The column family in HBase to write to.
AsyncHBaseSink	`asynchbase`	table: The name of the table in Hbase to write to. `columnFamily`: The column family in HBase to write to.

MorphlineSolrSink	`org.apache.`
	`flume.sink.`
	`solr.morphline.`
	`MorphlineSolrSink`
		`morphlineFile`: The relative or absolute path on the local file system to the morphline configuration file. Example: `/etc/flume-ng/conf/`
		`morphline.conf`

ElasticSearchSink	`org.apache.`
	`flume.sink.`
	`elasticsearch.`
	`ElasticSearchSink`
		`hostNames`: Comma separated list of hostname:port, if the port is not present the default port 9300 will be used

Example: For a sink that outputs to hdfs:

```
agent.sinks.log-hdfs.channel = channel1
agent.sinks.log-hdfs.type = hdfs
agent.sinks.log-hdfs.hdfs.path = hdfs://<server> /log/system.log/
```

Channels

Channels are temporary stores in an Agent, which can be used to hold the events received from the source and transfer the events to sink. Channels are typically of two forms:

- **In-Memory Queues**: These channels provides high throughput as data is not persisted due to which if an Agent fails, events are not recovered.

- **Disk-based Queues**: These channels provide full recovery even in case of event failure, but are a little slower than In-Memory due to the persistence of events.

Memory Channel, File Channel, and JDBC Channel are the three frequently used Flume Channels. We'll discuss them in the upcoming sections.

Memory channel

Memory channel stores events in an In-memory heap space. Memory channels are faster because of In-memory and as it won't persist the data to the disk. Memory channel should not be used if data loss is a concern because data will not be recovered if there is any crash in the process or machine. The properties that can be configured for defining Memory channel are:

- **type**: The value of the property should be `org.apache.flume.channel. MemoryChannel`.
- **capacity**: This is the maximum number of events the channel can hold. The default value is `100`.
- **transactionCapacity**: This is the maximum number of events that the source can send the events to the channel per transaction. The default value is `100`.
- **keep-alive**: This is the timeout period for adding and removing an event. The default value is `3`.
- **byteCapacity**: This is the maximum size of space allowed for the channel. The default value is 80 percent of the total heap memory allocated to the JVM.
- **byteCapacityBufferPercentage**: This is the percent age of buffer between the byte capacity of the channel and the total size of the bodies of all events currently in the channel. The default value is `20`.

File Channel

File channel persists the events on the disk and thus doesn't lose event data in case of a crash. File channels are used where data loss is not acceptable and to achieve reliability for processing. The configuration properties that can be set are:

- **type**: The value of the property should be `file`.
- **capacity**: The maximum number of events the channel can hold. The default value is `1000000`.
- **transactionCapacity**: The maximum number of events the source can send the events to the channel per transaction. The default value is `10000`.
- **checkpointDir**: The directory path where the checkpoint data should be saved.

- **dataDirs**: The directory where the data should be saved. The directories can be multiple and it can improve file channel performance.

- **useDualCheckpoints**: By default, the value of this property is `false`, which means checkpoint directory will not be backed up. If `true`, the checkpoint directory will be backed up.

- **backupCheckpointDir**: If `useDualCheckpoints` is true, the directory where the checkpoint should be saved.

- **checkpointInterval**: The time between the checkpoints.

- **maxFileSize**: The maximum size of a single log file. The default value is `2146435071`.

- **minimumRequiredSpace**: The minimum size below which the channel will stop operation to avoid data corruption. The default value is `524288000`.

- **keep-alive**: The timeout period for adding and removing an event. The default value is `3`.

JDBC Channel

JDBC channel persists the events in a database, and currently only derby database is supported. This channel can be used where the events should be recovered and all event processing is of utmost importance. The configuration properties to be set for JDBC channel are:

- **type**: The value of type should be `jdbc`.

- **db.type**: The type of database default to and currently only `DERBY` value that can be set.

- **driver.class**: The class for vendor JDBC driver. The default value is `org.apache.derby.jdbc.EmbeddedDriver`.

- **driver.url**: The connection url.

- **db.username**: The user ID of the database to connect.

Example:

```
db.password: password of the user id for database to connect.Example of a
Channel:agent.channels = c1

agent.channels.c1.type = memory

agent.channels.c1.capacity = 10000

agent.channels.c1.transactionCapacity = 10000

agent.channels.c1.byteCapacityBufferPercentage = 20

agent.channels.c1.byteCapacity = 800000
```

A simple Flume configuration can be represented by the following figure:

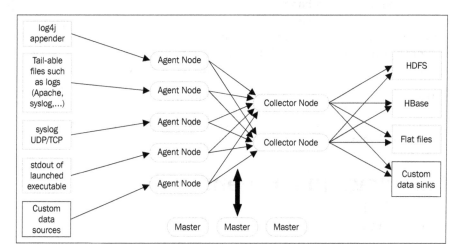

Examples of configuring Flume

Flume can be configured as a Single Agent or Multi Agent; we will see the respective examples in the upcoming sections.

The Single agent example

We will look at an example of the logger example and save it in HDFS and a memory channel, using the following code:

```
# Source of an Agent with tail
agent.source = source_log-tail
agent.sources.source_log-tail.type = exec
agent.sources.source_log-tail.command = tail -F /log/logger.log
agent.sources.source_log-tail.channels = memoryChannel

# Sink of an Agent to save in HDFS
agent.sinks = log-hdfs
agent.sinks.log-hdfs.channel = memoryChannel
agent.sinks.log-hdfs.type = hdfs
agent.sinks.log-hdfs.hdfs.path = /log/logger.log

# Channel of an Agent to store in memory
```

```
agent.channels = memoryChannel
agent.channels.memoryChannel.type = memory
agent.channels.memoryChannel.capacity = 10000
agent.channels.memoryChannel.transactionCapacity = 10000
agent.channels.memoryChannel.byteCapacityBufferPercentage = 20
agent.channels.memoryChannel.byteCapacity = 800000
```

Start the flume process, using the following command:

```
$ flume-ng agent -n agent -c conf -f conf/flume-conf.properties
  -Dflume.root.logger=INFO,console
```

Multiple flows in an agent

We can have multiple source, channel, and sink in an Agent configuration, using the following command:

```
<Agent>.sources = <Source1> <Source2>
```

```
<Agent>.sinks = <Sink1> <Sink2>
```

```
<Agent>.channels = <Channel1> <Channel2>
```

We can define the corresponding sources, sinks, and channels in the upcoming sections.

Configuring a multiagent setup

To configure a multi-agent setup, we have to link up the agents via an Avro/Thrift where an Avro sink type of one Agent acts as an Avro source type of another Agent. We should have two Agents. The first one will have a logger source and an Avro sink, which is shown in the following code:

```
# Source of an Agent with tail
agent1.source = source_log-tail
agent1.sources.source_log-tail.type = exec
agent1.sources.source_log-tail.command = tail -F /log/logger.log
agent1.sources.source_log-tail.channels = memoryChannel

agent1.sinks.avro-sink.type = avro
agent1.sinks.avro-sink.hostname = 192.168.0.1 #<hostname>
agent1.sinks.avro-sink.port = 1111

agent1.channels = memoryChannel
```

```
agent1.channels.memoryChannel.type = memory
agent1.channels.memoryChannel.capacity = 10000
agent1.channels.memoryChannel.transactionCapacity = 10000
agent1.channels.memoryChannel.byteCapacityBufferPercentage = 20
agent1.channels.memoryChannel.byteCapacity = 800000
```

The second Agent will have the Avro source of the first Agent sink:

```
# Source of an Agent with Avro source listening to sink of first Agent
agent2.source = avro-sink
agent2.sources.avro-sink.type = avro
agent2.sources.avro-sink.hostname = 192.168.0.1 #<hostname>
agent2.sources.avro-sink.port = 1111
agent2.sources.avro-sink.channels = memoryChannel


# Sink of an Agent to save in HDFS
agent2.sinks = log-hdfs
agent2.sinks.log-hdfs.channel = memoryChannel
agent2.sinks.log-hdfs.type = hdfs
agent2.sinks.log-hdfs.hdfs.path = /log/logger.log

agent2.channels = memoryChannel
agent2.channels.memoryChannel.type = memory
agent2.channels.memoryChannel.capacity = 10000
agent2.channels.memoryChannel.transactionCapacity = 10000
agent2.channels.memoryChannel.byteCapacityBufferPercentage = 20
agent2.channels.memoryChannel.byteCapacity = 800000
```

Start the flume agents in different nodes.

Start Agent2 in node 1, using the following command:

```
$ flume-ng agent -n agent2 -c conf -f conf/flume-conf.properties
  -Dflume.root.logger=INFO,console
```

Start Agent1 in node 2, using the following command:

```
$ flume-ng agent -n agent1 -c conf -f conf/flume-conf.properties
  -Dflume.root.logger=INFO,console
```

Summary

One of the critical phases of big data project is Data Ingestion, which we discussed. It is challenging and complex to develop and manage. Nowadays, data sources are in different formats and produce data in high velocity. We explored Sqoop and Flume architecture and its applications, in a nut shell.

We also learned how Sqoop provides a utility to import and export data between Hadoop and databases using connectors and drivers. Sqoop 1 is only JDBC based, and client-side responsibility and interoperability is limited code. Sqoop 2 is not only JDBC based, but also exposes restful API web-based architecture which is easily integrable.

Apache Flume is a reliable, flexible, customizable, and extensible framework to ingest data from fan in and fan out process. Flume has multitier topology, in which Agents can be configured to be used as Client, Collector, or Storage layer.

Hadoop was primarily a batch system, which has limited use cases and many big data use cases required for streaming data analysis and real-time capability. For processing real-time analysis, we will discuss Storm and Spark in the next chapter to process data effectively.

7
Streaming and Real-time Analysis – Storm and Spark

As we have already discussed about Hadoop being a Batch processing system and some data source types that varies in their velocity or rate, volume of data. Many system especially machines generates a lot of data consistently, they need to process such high volume data to maintain quality and avoid heavy loss and thus the need for Stream processing has emerged. To design systems that are built as Lambda implementation, which are Batch as well as Stream processing systems, We should have combination of different environment that can integrate with each other to process the data and quite obviously which increases the complexity of designing the system. Streaming data is complex to store, analyze, process, and maintain. Prior to version 2.*x*, Hadoop was only a Batch processing system, and after the emergence of YARN and other frameworks and the integration of those frameworks with YARN, Hadoop can be designed for streaming and real-time analysis with better performance. Various initiatives and contributions have elevated the capability of Hadoop with its integration with systems such as Storm and Spark.

In this chapter, we will cover the paradigms of Storm and Spark frameworks, in order to process streaming and conduct real-time analysis efficiently.

An introduction to Storm

Storm can process streaming data really fast (clocked at over one million messages per second per node); it is scalable (thousands of worker nodes of cluster), fault tolerant, and reliable (message processing is guaranteed). Storm is easy to use and deploy, which also eases its maintainability. Hadoop is primarily designed for batch processing and for Lambda Architecture systems. Storm is well-integrated with Hadoop, in order to provide distributed real-time streaming analysis reliably with good fault tolerance for big data.

Storm was developed by Twitter and later contributed to Apache. Storm's benchmark results are quite outstanding at over a million sets of data called tuples processed per second per node. Storm utilizes a Thrift interface; hence, the client can be written in any language and even non-JVM language communicates over JSON-based protocol. Considering the complexity of Storm, it is a fairly easy-to-use API.

Features of Storm

Some important features of Storm are as follows:

- Simple programming model
- Free and open source
- Can be used with any language
- Fault-tolerant
- Distributed and horizontally scalable—runs across a cluster of machines in parallel
- Reliable—guaranteed message processing
- Fast—processes streaming data in real time
- Easy to deploy and operate

Physical architecture of Storm

Storm architecture is based on the master-slave model and utilizes Zookeeper for coordination between the master and slaves. It is composed of four components:

- **Nimbus**: Master process that distributes processing across clusters
- **Supervisor**: Manages worker nodes
- **Worker**: Executes tasks assigned by Nimbus
- **Zookeeper**: Coordinates between Nimbus and Supervisors

Workers send heartbeats to **Supervisors** and **Nimbus** via **Zookeeper**. If a **Worker** or **Supervisor** is not able to respond, then **Nimbus** reassigns the work to another node in the cluster, which is shown in the following figure:

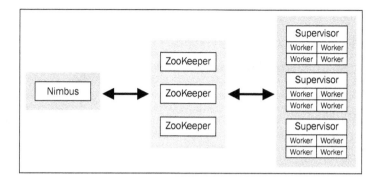

Data architecture of Storm

Storm data architecture has the following terminologies:

- **Spout**: Produces Stream or data source
- **Bolt**: Ingests the Spout tuples then processes it and produces output stream; it can be used to filter, aggregate, or join data, or talk to databases
- **Topology**: A network graph between Spouts and Bolts

The following figure explains the preceding points:

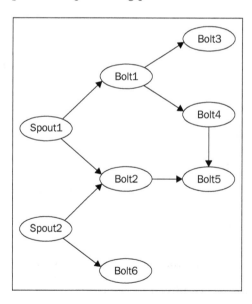

The data level abstractions in Storm are:

- **Tuple**: The basic unit of Storm data—a named list of values
- **Stream**: An unbounded sequence of tuples

The following figure shows the spouts producing streams and bolts processing the tuples or streams to produce different streams:

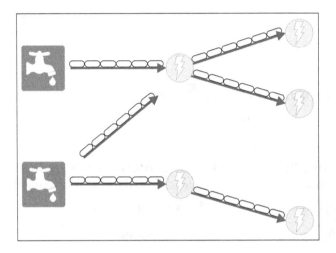

Storm topology

Streams can be partitioned among bolts by using stream grouping, which allows the streams to be routed towards a bolt. Storm provides the following built-in stream groupings, and you can implement a custom stream grouping by implementing the interface:

- **Shuffle grouping**: Each bolt is configured uniformly to get an almost equal number of tuples
- **Fields grouping**: Grouping on a particular field is possible to consolidate the tuples of the same field value and different value tuples to different bolts
- **All grouping**: Each tuple can be sent to all the bolts but can increase the overhead
- **Global grouping**: All the tuples go to a single bolt
- **Direct grouping**: The producer can decide which tuples to be sent to which bolt

Storm on YARN

Storm integration on YARN was done in Yahoo and released as an open source. Storm can be integrated with YARN to provide batch and real-time analysis on the same cluster as Lambda architecture. Storm on YARN couples Storm's event-processing framework with Hadoop to provide low latency processing. Storm resources can be managed by YARN to provide all the benefits of stream processing by Storm on Hadoop. Storm on YARN provides high availability, optimization, and elasticity in resource utilization.

Topology configuration example

Storm topology can be configured by the TopologyBuilder class by creating spouts and bolts, and then by submitting the topology.

Spouts

Some implementations of spouts are available in Storm, such as **BaseRichSpout, ClojureSpout, DRPCSpout, FeederSpout, FixedTupleSpout, MasterBatchCoordinator, RichShellSpout, RichSpoutBatchTriggerer, ShellSpout, SpoutTracker, TestPlannerSpout, TestWordSpout,** and **TransactionalSpoutCoordinator.**

We can write a custom bolts by extending any of the aforementioned classes or implementing the ISpout interface:

```
public class NumberSpout extends BaseRichSpout
{
    private SpoutOutputCollector collector;

    private static int currentNumber = 1;

    @Override
    public void open( Map conf, TopologyContext context,
SpoutOutputCollector collector )
    {
        this.collector = collector;
    }

    @Override
    public void nextTuple()
```

```
        {

            // Emit the next number
            collector.emit( new Values( new Integer( currentNumber++ ) )
    );
        }

        @Override
        public void ack(Object id)
        {
        }

        @Override
        public void fail(Object id)
        {
        }

        @Override
        public void declareOutputFields(OutputFieldsDeclarer declarer)
        {
            declarer.declare( new Fields( "number" ) );
        }
    }
```

Bolts

Some implementations of bolts are available in Storm, such as **BaseBasicBolt**,
BatchProcessWord, **BatchRepeatA**, **IdentityBolt**, **PrepareBatchBolt**, **PrepareRequest**,
TestConfBolt, **TestWordCounter**, and **TridentSpoutCoordinator**.

We can write a custom bolt by extending any of the aforementioned classes
or implementing the IBasicBolt interface:

```
public class PrimeNumberBolt extends BaseRichBolt
{
  private OutputCollector collector;
  public void prepare( Map conf, TopologyContext context,
OutputCollector collector )
  {
    this.collector = collector;
```

```java
  }

  public void execute( Tuple tuple )
  {
    int number = tuple.getInteger( 0 );
    if( isPrime( number) )
    {
      System.out.println( number );
    }
    collector.ack( tuple );
  }

  public void declareOutputFields( OutputFieldsDeclarer declarer )
  {
    declarer.declare( new Fields( "number" ) );
  }

  private boolean isPrime( int n )
  {
    if( n == 1 || n == 2 || n == 3 )
    {
      return true;
    }
    // Is n an even number?
    if( n % 2 == 0 )
    {
      return false;
    }

        //if not, then just check the odds
        for( int i=3; i*i<=n; i+=2 )
        {
            if( n % i == 0)
            {
                return false;
            }
        }
        return true;
  }
}
```

Topology

The `TopologyBuilder` class can be used to configure the spouts and bolts and to submit the topology, as shown in this example:

```
public class PrimeNumberTopology
{
  public static void main(String[] args)
  {
    TopologyBuilder builder = new TopologyBuilder();
    builder.setSpout( "spout", new NumberSpout() );
    builder.setBolt( "prime", new PrimeNumberBolt() )
    .shuffleGrouping("spout");

    Config conf = new Config();
    LocalCluster cluster = new LocalCluster();
    cluster.submitTopology("test", conf,
      builder.createTopology());
    Utils.sleep(10000);
    cluster.killTopology("test");
    cluster.shutdown();
  }
}
```

An introduction to Spark

Spark is a cluster computing framework, which was developed in AMPLab at UC Berkley and contributed as an open source project to Apache. Spark is an in-memory based data processing framework, which makes it much faster in processing than MapReduce. In MapReduce, intermediate data is stored in the disk and data access and transfer makes it slower, whereas in Spark it is stored in-memory. Spark can be thought of as an alternative to MapReduce due to the limitations and overheads of the latter, but not as a replacement. Spark is widely used for streaming data analytics, graph analytics, fast interactive queries, and machine learning. It has attracted the attention of many contributors due to its in-memory nature and actually was one of the top-level Apache projects in 2014 with over 200 contributors and 50+ organizations. Spark utilizes multiple threads instead of multiple processes to achieve parallelism on a single node.

Spark's main motive was to develop a processing system that would be faster and easier to use and could be used for analytics. Its programming follows more of the **Directed Acyclic Graph (DAG)** pattern, in which multi-step data flows and is complex, which is explained in the following figure:

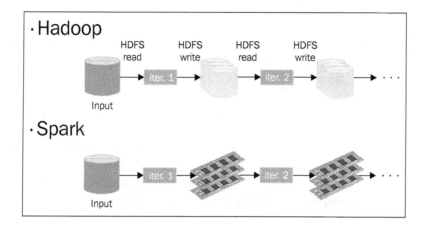

Features of Spark

Spark has numerous features and capabilities worth mentioning, as follows:

- Runs 100 times faster than MapReduce when running in-memory and 10 times faster when running on disk

- Can process iterative and interactive analytics

- Many functions and operators available for data analysis

- DAG framework to design functions easily

- In-memory based intermediate storage

- Easy to use and maintain

- Written in Scala and runs in JVM environment; applications using Spark can be written in Scala, Java, Python, R, Clojure

- Runs in environments such as Hadoop and Mesos, or standalone, or in cloud

Spark framework

Spark contributors have utilized the core Spark framework and have developed different libraries on top of Spark to enhance its capabilities. These libraries can be plugged in to Spark as per the requirement:

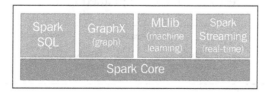

Spark SQL

Spark SQL is a wrapper of SQL on top of Spark. It transforms SQL queries into Spark jobs to produce results. Spark SQL can work with a variety of data sources, such as Hive tables, Parquet files, and JSON files.

GraphX

GraphX, as the name suggests, enables working with graph-based algorithms. It has a wide variety of graph-based algorithms already implemented and is still growing. Some examples are PageRank, Connected components, Label propagation, SVD++, strongly connected components, Triangle count, and so on.

MLib

MLib is a scalable machine learning library that works on top of Spark. It is considerably easier to use and deploy, and its performance can be optimized to be 100 times faster than MapReduce.

Spark streaming

Spark streaming is a library that enables Spark to perform scalable, fault-tolerant, high throughput system to process streaming data in real time. Spark Streaming is well integrated with many sources, such as **Kinesis**, **HDFS**, **S3**, **Flume**, **Kafka**, **Twitter**, and so on, which is shown in the following figure:

Spark streaming can be integrated with MLib and GraphX to process their algorithms or libraries in streaming data. Spark streaming ingests the input data from a source and breaks it into batches. The batch is stored as an internal dataset (RDD—we will look at it in detail) for processing, which is explained in the following figure:

Spark architecture

Spark architecture is based on a DAG engine and its data model works on **Resilient Distributed Dataset (RDD)**, which is its USP with a large number of benefits in terms of performance. In Spark the computations are performed lazily, which allows the DAG engine to identify the step or computation that is not needed for the end result and is not performed at all, thus improving performance.

Directed Acyclic Graph engine

Spark has an advanced DAG engine that manages the data flow. A job in Spark is transformed in a DAG with task stages and the graph is then optimized. The tasks identified are then analyzed to check if they can be processed in one stage or multiple stages. Task locality is also analyzed to optimize the process.

Resilient Distributed Dataset

As per the white paper "Resilient Distributed Datasets, a Fault-Tolerant Abstraction for In-Memory Cluster Computing." Matei Zaharia, Mosharaf Chowdhury, Tathagata Das, Ankur Dave, Justin Ma, Murphy McCauley, Michael J. Franklin, Scott Shenker, Ion Stoica on April 2012. This paper has also received Best Paper Award and Honorable Mention for Community Award. An RDD is a read-only, partitioned collection of records. RDDs can only be created through deterministic operations on either (a) data in stable storage or (b) other RDDs.

RDDs are an 'immutable resilient distributed collection of records, which can be stored in the volatile memory or in a persistent storage (HDFS, HBase, and so on) and can be converted into another RDD through some transformations. An RDD stores the data in-memory as long as possible. If the data grows larger than the threshold, it spills into the disk. Due to this, the computation becomes faster. On the other hand, if some node holding the data in memory fails, then that part of computations has to be processed again. To avoid this, check pointing is performed after some stages, which is shown in the following figure:

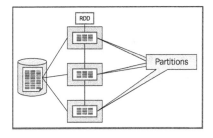

RDDs are of two types:

- **Parallelized collections**: Created by invoking SparkContext's parallelize method
- **Hadoop datasets**: Created from HDFS files

An RDD can perform either transformation or actions. Transformations can be used for some filters or map functions. Actions can return a value after some executions, such as reduce or count.

An RDD can have two types of dependencies: narrow and wide. Narrow dependencies occur when a partition of an RDD is used by only one partition of the next RDD. Wide dependencies occur when a partition of an RDD is used by multiple partitions in the next RDD usually in groups and joins. The following figure shows the two types of dependencies:

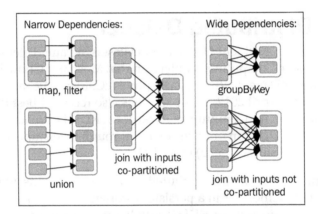

The features of RDDs are as follows:

- Resilient and fault tolerant; in case of any failure they can be rebuilt according to the data stored
- Distributed
- Datasets partitioned across cluster nodes
- Immutable
- Memory-intensive
- Caching levels configurable according to the environment

Physical architecture

Spark's physical architecture components are composed of Spark Master and Spark Worker, where as Hadoop Spark Worker sits on the data nodes. Spark Master controls the workflow and it is highly available on top of YARN. We can configure a backup Spark Master for easy failover. Spark Worker launches appropriate executors for each task, which is shown in the following figure:

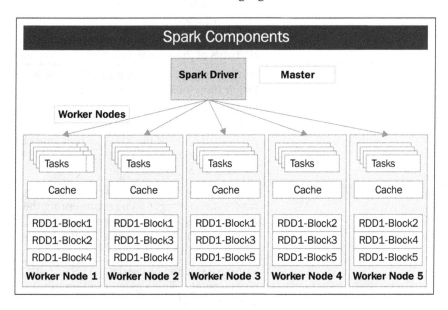

In deployment, one analytics node runs the Spark Master, and Spark Workers run on each of the nodes.

Operations in Spark

RDDs support two types of operations:

* Transformations
* Actions

Transformations

The transformation operation performs some functions and creates another dataset. Transformations are processed in the lazy mode and only those transformations that are needed in the end result are processed. If any transformation is found unnecessary, then Spark ignores it, and this improves the efficiency.

Transformations, which are available and mentioned in Spark Apache docs at `https://spark.apache.org/docs/latest/programming-guide.html#transformations`, are as follows:

Transformation	Meaning
`map (func)`	Return a new distributed dataset formed by passing each element of the source through a function `func`.
`filter (func)`	Return a new dataset formed by selecting those elements of the source on which `func` returns true.
`flatMap (func)`	Similar to map, but each input item can be mapped to 0 or more output items (so `func` should return a `Seq` rather than a single item).
`mapPartitions (func)`	Similar to map, but runs separately on each partition (block) of the RDD, so func must be of type `Iterator[T]` => `Iterator[U]` when running on an RDD of type T.
`mapPartitionsWithSplit (func)`	Similar to mapPartitions, but also provides func with an integer value representing the index of the split, so func must be of type (`Int`, `Iterator[T]`) => `Iterator[U]` when running on an RDD of type T.
`Sample (withReplacement,fraction, seed)`	Sample a fraction of the data, with or without replacement, using a given random number generator seed.
`Union (otherDataset)`	Return a new dataset that contains the union of the elements in the source dataset and the argument.
`Distinct ([numTasks]))`	Return a new dataset that contains the distinct elements of the source dataset.
`groupByKey ([numTasks])`	When called on a dataset of (K, V) pairs, returns a dataset of (K, Seq[V]) pairs. Note: By default, this uses only eight parallel tasks to do the grouping. You can pass an optional `numTasks` argument to set a different number of tasks.
`reduceByKey (func, [numTasks])`	When called on a dataset of (K, V) pairs, returns a dataset of (K, V) pairs where the values of each key are aggregated using the given reduce function. Like in groupByKey, the number of reduce tasks is configurable through an optional second argument.

Transformation	Meaning
sortByKey ([ascending], [numTasks])	When called on a dataset of (K, V) pairs where K implements Ordered, returns a dataset of (K, V) pairs, sorted by keys in ascending or descending order, as specified in the Boolean ascending argument.
Join (otherDataset, [numTasks])	When called on datasets of type (K, V) and (K, W), returns a dataset of (K, (V, W)) pairs with all pairs of elements for each key.
Cogroup (otherDataset, [numTasks])	When called on datasets of type (K, V) and (K, W), returns a dataset of (K, Seq[V], Seq[W]) tuples. This operation is also called **groupWith**.
Cartesian (otherDataset)	When called on datasets of types T and U, returns a dataset of (T, U) pairs (all pairs of elements).

Actions

Action operations produce and return a result. An action's result is actually written to an external storage system. Actions available and mentioned in Spark Apache docs, mentioned at `https://spark.apache.org/docs/latest/programming-guide.html#actions` are as follows:

Action	Meaning
Reduce (func)	Aggregate the elements of the dataset using a function func (which takes two arguments and returns one). The function should be commutative and associative, so that it can be computed correctly in parallel.
Collect ()	Return all the elements of the dataset as an array at the driver program. This is usually useful after a filter or other operation that returns a sufficiently small subset of the data.
Count ()	Return the number of elements in the dataset.
First ()	Return the first element of the dataset (similar to take(1)).
Take (n)	Return an array with the first n elements of the dataset. Note that this is currently not executed in parallel. Instead, the driver program computes all the elements.

Action	Meaning
`takeSample (withReplacement,num, seed)`	Return an array with a random sample of num elements of the dataset, with or without replacement, using the given random number generator seed.
`saveAsTextFile (path)`	Write the elements of the dataset as a text file (or set of text files) in a given directory in the local filesystem, HDFS, or any other Hadoop-supported file system. Spark will call `toString` on each element to convert it to a line of text in the file.
`saveAsSequenceFile (path)`	Write the elements of the dataset as a Hadoop SequenceFile in a given path in the local filesystem, HDFS, or any other Hadoop-supported file system. This is only available on RDDs of key-value pairs that either implement Hadoop's Writable interface or are implicitly convertible to Writable (Spark includes conversions for basic types like Int, Double, String, and so on).
`countByKey ()`	Only available on RDDs of type (K, V). Returns a Map of (K, Int) pairs with the count of each key.
`Foreach (func)`	Run a function `func` on each element of the dataset. This is usually done for side effects such as updating an accumulator variable (see below) or interacting with external storage systems.

Spark example

For simplicity, let's take Word count as an example in Spark.

In Scala:

```scala
val file = spark.textFile("hdfs://...")
val counts = file.flatMap(line => line.split(" "))
  .map(word => (word, 1))
  .reduceByKey(_ + _)
counts.saveAsTextFile("hdfs://...")
```

In Java:

```
JavaRDD<String> file =
  spark.textFile("hdfs://...");JavaRDD<String> words =
    file.flatMap(new FlatMapFunction<String, String>() {
  public Iterable<String> call(String s) {
return Arrays.asList(s.split(" ")); }
});

JavaPairRDD<String, Integer> pairs = words.mapToPair(new
  PairFunction<String, String, Integer>() {
    public Tuple2<String, Integer> call(String s) {
return new Tuple2<String, Integer>(s, 1); }});

JavaPairRDD<String, Integer> counts = pairs.reduceByKey(new
  Function2<Integer, Integer>() {
  public Integer call(Integer a, Integer b) {
return a + b; }});
counts.saveAsTextFile("hdfs://...");
```

Summary

Streaming and real-time analysis are required in many systems in big data. Batch processing is very well handled by Hadoop and integration of frameworks like Storm and Spark elevates their streaming and real-time capability.

We discussed that Storm is an open source, fast, stream processing, scalable, fault-tolerant, and reliable system that is easy to use and deploy. Storm's physical architecture comprises Nimbus, Supervisor, Worker, and Zookeeper processes. The data architecture of Storm comprises a spouts, bolts, and topology-based data flow system.

Spark is an extremely popular framework which provides in-memory data handling capability and makes it much faster than the MapReduce framework. Spark frameworks have some libraries such as Spark SQL, GraphX, MLib, Spark Streaming, and others to process specialized data and requirements. Spark Architecture is based on RDDs and the DAG engine, which provides capability of in-memory data processing and optimizes the processing, according to the data flow effectively and efficiently. Spark RDD can perform numerous transformations and actions.

Finally, we have come to the last chapter and have covered different sets of tools and utilities within the Hadoop Ecosystem. I hope that the book will be useful to you and give you a quick heads-up about the components and essential details, as well as how to use them.

Index

Thank you for buying
Hadoop Essentials

About Packt Publishing

Packt, pronounced 'packed', published its first book, *Mastering phpMyAdmin for Effective MySQL Management*, in April 2004, and subsequently continued to specialize in publishing highly focused books on specific technologies and solutions.

Our books and publications share the experiences of your fellow IT professionals in adapting and customizing today's systems, applications, and frameworks. Our solution-based books give you the knowledge and power to customize the software and technologies you're using to get the job done. Packt books are more specific and less general than the IT books you have seen in the past. Our unique business model allows us to bring you more focused information, giving you more of what you need to know, and less of what you don't.

Packt is a modern yet unique publishing company that focuses on producing quality, cutting-edge books for communities of developers, administrators, and newbies alike. For more information, please visit our website at www.packtpub.com.

Writing for Packt

We welcome all inquiries from people who are interested in authoring. Book proposals should be sent to author@packtpub.com. If your book idea is still at an early stage and you would like to discuss it first before writing a formal book proposal, then please contact us; one of our commissioning editors will get in touch with you.

We're not just looking for published authors; if you have strong technical skills but no writing experience, our experienced editors can help you develop a writing career, or simply get some additional reward for your expertise.

Mastering Hadoop

ISBN: 978-1-78398-364-3   Paperback: 374 pages

Go beyond the basics and master the next generation of Hadoop data processing platforms

1. Learn how to optimize Hadoop MapReduce, Pig and Hive.

2. Dive into YARN and learn how it can integrate Storm with Hadoop.

3. Understand how Hadoop can be deployed on the cloud and gain insights into analytics with Hadoop.

Building Hadoop Clusters [Video]

ISBN: 978-1-78328-403-0   Duration: 02:34 hrs

Deploy multi-node Hadoop clusters to harness the Cloud for storage and large-scale data processing

1. Familiarize yourself with Hadoop and its services, and how to configure them.

2. Deploy compute instances and set up a three-node Hadoop cluster on Amazon.

3. Set up a Linux installation optimized for Hadoop.

Please check **www.PacktPub.com** for information on our titles

Big Data Analytics with R and Hadoop

ISBN: 978-1-78216-328-2   Paperback: 238 pages

Set up an integrated infrastructure of R and Hadoop to turn your data analytics into Big Data analytics

1. Write Hadoop MapReduce within R.

2. Learn data analytics with R and the Hadoop platform.

3. Handle HDFS data within R.

4. Understand Hadoop streaming with R.

Hadoop Beginner's Guide

ISBN: 978-1-84951-730-0   Paperback: 398 pages

Learn how to crunch big data to extract meaning from the data avalanche

1. Learn tools and techniques that let you approach big data with relish and not fear.

2. Shows how to build a complete infrastructure to handle your needs as your data grows.

3. Hands-on examples in each chapter give the big picture while also giving direct experience.

Please check **www.PacktPub.com** for information on our titles

www.ingramcontent.com/pod-product-compliance
Lightning Source LLC
Chambersburg PA
CBHW060130060326
40690CB00018B/3817